THE PUNJAB STORY

Other Lotus Titles

Frank Simoes	*Frank Unedited*
Frank Simoes	*Frank Simoes' Goa*
Harinder Baweja (ed.)	*Most Wanted: Profiles of Terror*
J.N. Dixit (ed.)	*External Affairs: Cross-Border Relations*
Khushwant Singh	*Death at My Doorstep*
M.J. Akbar	*India: The Siege Within*
M.J. Akbar	*Kashmir: Behind the Vale*
M.J. Akbar	*Nehru: The Making of India*
M.J. Akbar	*Riot after Riot*
M.J. Akbar	*The Shade of Swords*
M.J. Akbar	*By Line*
Meghnad Desai	*Nehru's Hero Dilip Kumar: In the Life of India*
Nayantara Sahgal	*Before Freedom: Nehru's Letters to His Sister*
Rohan Gunaratna	*Inside Al Qaeda*
Rifaat Hussain, J.N. Dixit Julie Sirrs, Ajai Shukla Anand Giridharadas Rahimullah Yusufzai John Jennings	*Afghanistan and 9/11*
Eric S. Margolis	*War at the Top of the World*
Maj. Gen. Ian Cardozo	*Param Vir: Our Heroes in Battle*
Mushirul Hasan	*India Partitioned. 2 Vols*
Mushirul Hasan	*John Company to the Republic*
Mushirul Hasan	*Knowledge Power and Politics*
Prafulla Roy, trans. John W.Hood	*In the Shadow of the Sun*
Rachel Dwyer	*Yash Chopra: Fifty Years of Indian Cinema*
Satish Jacob	*From Hotel Palestine Baghdad*
Sujata S. Sabnis	*A Twist in Destiny*
V.N. Rai	*Curfew in the City*
Veena Sharma	*Kailash Mansarovar: A Sacred Journey*

Forthcoming Titles :

Maj. R.P. Singh, Kanwar Rajpal Singh	Sawai Man Singh of Jaipur Life and Legend
Premchand trans. Madan Gopal	My Life and Times: An Autobiographical Narative
Vaibhav Purandare	*Sachin Tendulkar: A Biography*

THE PUNJAB STORY

AMARJIT KAUR
LT. GEN. J S AURORA
KHUSHWANT SINGH
M V KAMATH
SHEKHAR GUPTA
SUBHASH KIRPEKAR
SUNIL SETHI
TAVLEEN SINGH

FOREWORD BY
KPS GILL

LOTUS COLLECTION
ROLI BOOKS

Lotus Collection

First published in hardback in 1984 by
Roli Books International

Second edition published in 2004
Third impression in 2005
The Lotus Collection
An imprint of
Roli Books Pvt. Ltd.
M-75, G.K. II Market, New Delhi 110 048
Phones: ++91 (011) 2921 2271, 2921 2782
2921 0886, Fax: ++91 (011) 2921 7185
E-mail: roli@vsnl.com; Website: rolibooks.com
Also at
Varanasi, Agra, Jaipur and the Netherlands

Cover design: Arati Subramanyam

ISBN: 81-7436-331-9
Rs 295

Typeset in Minion by Roli Books Pvt. Ltd. and
printed at Tan Prints (India) Pvt. Ltd., Jhajjar, Haryana

CONTENTS

Publisher's Note

Unprecedented in the history of India, the happenings in Punjab in the 1980s have scarred the face of a nation otherwise known for its unity in diversity. The injury inflicted by the secessionists' demands and the senseless killings were thought to have been cured by the surgical operation which the government carried out in the form of Operation Bluestar in early June 1984. Whether this operation succeeded in achieving its objective is best judged by people who had set the objectives before embarking on it. However, having performed the operation successfully, the government did feel the need for a healing touch.

Punjab then was a major issue and continued to be a point of great debate in the country for some time to come. Many questions were asked: whether the army action was necessary? What was the situation that led to the army operation? Will the healing touch work? Also many rumours were in the air. One man plays up the other man's statements. Facts become fiction. Most often this is unintentional. The aim of the present volume was to clear the misunderstandings between the two communities of Punjab and bring peace and amity among them.

The Punjab Story attempts to organize a symposium of a group of people who have closely watched and studied the Punjab scenario. Each contributor to this volume has been actively and closely associated with the Punjab issue – whether in protest or in agreement with the government. This book also tries to put forward independent views of eight eminent personalities. The effort is to bring out facts as experienced by these eight contributors and put them in the form of a debate before the reader.

Among the contributors, Smt Amarjit Kaur, then a Member of Parliament, belonging to a former royal Sikh family came out very openly and convincingly for the stand taken by the government. On the contrary, Khushwant Singh, then also a Sikh Member of Parliament, who was on the extremists' hit list because of his criticism of Bhindranwale, shares his emotions with most Sikhs.

M.V. Kamath, another veteran journalist, felt a sinister movement for Khalistan in the Shiromani Gurdwara Parbandhak Committee (SGPC) when he visited Amritsar way back in 1979 as editor of the *Illustrated Weekly of India* to do a cover story on the Golden Temple. Through the military mind of Lt Gen J.S. Aurora of the Bangladesh War fame, the reader gets to know of the tactical, strategical, and executionary flaws of the army operation.

The scenes of the battle are described by two brave journalists Shekhar Gupta and Subhash Kirpekar whose eyewitness accounts, coupled with scores of the army contacts that they were able to establish, enable them to provide blow by blow accounts. They were perhaps the only journalists to be so closely watching the drama that was Operation Bluestar.

Tavleen Singh, the fiery young journalist who has been covering Punjab since early 1980s, had some of the most stunning interviews with the extremists stored in her cassettes which she has revealed in her article.

Sunil Sethi was born and brought up in Amritsar. He travelled extensively throughout Punjab during the last few years and came up with a moving story on the great divide between the Sikhs and non-Sikhs in the state.

Finally, the government's point of view is expressed here in the form of a summary of the White Paper on Punjab.

Foreword

Two decades have passed since the vast upsurge of violence in Punjab – the Sikh fundamentalist terrorist movement for 'Khalistan' – was quelled. The comprehensive defeat of this terrorist movement is unique in history, leaving behind no ideological lees, no residual rage, no reservoir of sullen hostility. Again and again, since 1993, Pakistan has sought to revive the movement, and has successfully engineered a handful of random incidents, ordinarily against soft targets, but has failed utterly in touching a sympathetic chord among the people of Punjab, particularly the Jat Sikhs, among whom, at one time, the extremists found a majority of their recruits – as, in fact, did the police and security forces.

Indeed, if any evidence of the Khalistani fervour survives, it is among a handful of lunatic expatriates, entirely divorced from the realities of the ground in Punjab. Even this lunatic fringe has been shedding regularly, as some of its leading oddballs crawl shamefacedly back into the country to 'rejoin the mainstream.' Others continue to rant ineffectually in their safe havens in Pakistan, or in their adopted countries abroad, increasingly discredited among those who lent them some credence in the past.

Punjab's recovery from the years of violence has, in many ways, been miraculous. The latter half of the 1990s saw an unprecedented cultural resurgence, one that impacted, through a new range of mass media and television channels, on the entire country. The spirit of Punjab, its economic dynamism, and the will of the people appeared to have emerged unscathed from the trial by fire over nearly a decade and a half of terrorism.

Over this period of the Punjabi revival, I was often asked whether terrorism could ever return to the state, and my answer, invariably, was confidently in the negative. The sheer totality of the defeat of the terrorist forces, in combination with the attendant atmosphere of social, cultural and economic renaissance that followed it, convinced me that the people of Punjab would never allow the nightmare to be repeated again.

Today, I am not as certain of this as I was some years ago. Punjab has, for the past decade, been outrageously misgoverned, with incompetence and rampant corruption standing out as the hallmarks of the successive regimes that have inflicted immense damage on the state since the end of terrorism. Among the worst affected by the irresponsibility and venality of succeeding administrations, have been the Jat Sikh farmers, and at least some among these proud people have been driven to suicide by debt and a deteriorating rural economy. The resolution they seek to their problems, nevertheless, still lies fully within the democratic political order – despite its attendant frustrations – and the militancy of the past finds no supporters today. But the rampant corruption, ineptitude and lack of imagination that has characterized the political and bureaucratic establishments in successive administrations, cutting across party lines, since the assassination of chief minister Beant Singh, and the continuing failure to meet even the minimal aspirations of the young and underprivileged, now make it difficult to entirely exclude the possibility of a revival of the politics of extremism and violence, though such an eventuality may not be realized in the near future.

It is useful at this time, consequently, to remind ourselves that it was precisely this pattern of venality and neglect, combined with some of the gravest and most unprincipled political misadventures by the leadership of that time – both at the state and national level – that had given rise to the terror towards the end of the 1970s. For many, it is still a matter of complete amazement that Punjab, with its booming economy and a people so generous and open-hearted, could have been seduced by the narrow-minded and mean-spirited ideology of communal ghettoization that went by the name of 'Khalistan.' But those who have closely studied the dynamic of the emergence and consolidation of the terror in the early 1980s will understand that a comparable failure of political imagination, in combination with a sustained pattern of administrative incompetence and cynical manipulation, can bring about future disasters as well.

Looking back today, the terrorism of those early years appears simple and unthreatening, compared with what was to follow, and one wonders at the myth-making that created the immensely larger-than-life image of Jarnail Singh Bhindranwale. In hindsight, Operation Bluestar was possibly the single most significant act of political overreaction and military incompetence that gave a lease of life to a movement that could easily have been ended in the mid-1980s. The redundancy of Operation Bluestar was, in any event, demonstrated in 1988, when Operation Black Thunder – originally called the Gill Plan by Rajiv Gandhi, when I first outlined it to him at his residential office, and which was accepted by him in toto – once again defenestrated the Golden Temple of the terrorist presence, this time without the disastrous consequences that Bluestar had provoked. Black Thunder and the counter-terrorism campaign that followed put the terrorists to flight by the end of 1989; but politics intervened once again, and vacillation, the failure of political imagination, and the outright incompetence of the national leadership at the highest level, again wasted the advantage that had been gained through the enormous sacrifices of the security forces. Thousands of lives were still to be lost on both sides of the battlelines before sense eventually prevailed, and the last phase of the counter-insurgency campaign brought the terrorists to their final defeat.

And yet, twenty years after Bluestar, and more than a decade after peace was restored to Punjab, the state has little to show for those thousands of lives wasted on both sides of the conflict. Punjab and the Punjabis today appear to have been cast into an endless political purgatory, with the same discredited leadership that led them into the torments of the 1980s and the early 1990s resurfacing. Nowhere on the political horizon is there any sign of political vision or of a leadership that could steer the destinies of the state in a direction that conforms to the aspirations of its people. And the expectations of the people of Punjab far outstrip not only the vision of their leaders, but possibly the highest aspirations of any other people in the country. The Punjabi seeks a level of prosperity that would not even be imagined by most other people in India. And the growing hiatus between these burgeoning expectations, and the capacity of the political and administrative system to meet them, is a matter for great and immediate concern.

There has been little serious effort to examine and understand the contours of the very complex Punjab experience – both at its best and its worst. In the absence of such examination and understanding, there is little hope of transformation. The present collection of writings reflects the direct experience of those who lived through the terror in Punjab. To this extent, it may be coloured by their proximity to those historical and troubling events. This immediacy, however, lends the writings in this volume an authenticity and worth that would be difficult to locate in the works of academics, distanced from the events they analyze. This volume is a record of history in the making, and is consequently indispensable for anyone who seeks to understand the 'troubles' in Punjab.

K.P.S. Gill
New Delhi, June 2004

Genesis of the Hindu-Sikh Divide

KHUSHWANT SINGH

Sikhism was born out of Hinduism. All the ten Sikh gurus were Hindus till they became Sikhs. The Granth Sahib which Sikhs regard as the 'Living Light' of their gurus can be described as the essence of Vedanta. Nevertheless like other reformist movements Sikhism broke away from its parent Hindu body and evolved its own distinct rites of worship and ritual, its own code of ethics, its separate traditions which cumulatively gave it a distinct religious personality

The founder of the Sikh faith, Guru Nanak (AD 1469-1539) was a Kshatriya of the Bedi (those who know the vedas) sub-caste. When he was 30 years old he had a mystic experience after which he announced his mission with the simple statement: 'there is no Hindu, there is no Mussalman.' The statement could be interpreted in different ways. It could mean that there were no basic differences between Hinduism and Islam. Or that followers of neither religion were true to their faiths. Or that all human beings were the same and dividing them into different religions was pointless. However, during the same mystic experience, Guru Nanak is said to have received orders from God to preach a new faith: 'Nanak, I am with thee. Through thee will My Name be magnified. Go into the world and teach mankind how to pray. Be not sullied by the ways of the world, let your life be one of praise of the word *(naam)*, charity (*daan*), ablution (*ishnaan*), service (*seva*) and prayer (*simran*).' Guru Nanak spent the remaining years of his life travelling to different parts of India and West Asia. His last years were spent in village Kartarpur where he set up a *dharamsala* (place of religion). Large numbers of peasants became his *shishyas* (disciples) from which the word Sikh is derived. For his rustic followers he summed up his message in three simple commandments: *kirt karo* (work), *naam japo* (worship) and *wand chako* (share what you earn).

The way of life Guru Nanak recommended was somewhat different from that of the Hindus and Muslims. He emphasized the role of truthful companionship (*satsangi*) which was interpreted as the company of those who accepted Nanak's teaching. The breakaway from Hinduism began by having different places and modes of worship. Sikhs did not chant Sanskrit *shlokas* to stone idols but sang hymns composed by Nanak in his own mother tongue, Punjabi. Sikhs broke bread in the guru's kitchen (*guru ka langar)* where men and women of different castes including Harijans sat alongside and ate together. They did not use Hindu greetings like namaskar or *jai* Ram *ji ki* but their guru's *Sat Kartar* (True Creator). All this resulted in building a community of people who had more in common with each other than to other communities to which they had belonged.

It is still disputed whether Guru Nanak intended to reform Hinduism, form a third community or bring Hindus and Muslims together. It would appear that in his earlier career he tried to bring the two communities closer to each other. Being himself a Hindu he was at the same time equally concerned with reforming Hinduism. But as the years went by and his message caught on among the masses, he decided to give his teachings permanency through a sect of his own.

The process of separation was carried a step further by Guru Nanak's chief disciple, Angad, who succeeded him as the second guru. He evolved a new script, Gurmukhi, in which he compiled his mentor's and his own compositions. The third Guru, Amar Das, introduced many innovations which tended to break the close affiliations of the Sikhs with the Hindus. He fixed the first of Baisakh as a day of general assembly for the Sikhs, introduced new forms of ceremonies for births, deaths and marriages and selected hymns to be chanted on these occasions. He abolished the practice of *purdah,* advocated monogamy, encouraged inter-caste alliances, remarriage of widows and forbade *sati.* Guru Amar Das's son-in-law, Ram Das, who succeeded him as the fourth guru, acquired the site of the present city of Amritsar and had a tank dug around which bazaars went up. His son and successor, Guru Arjun, raised the Harmandir in the midst of this tank. It was Arjun who made the first clear statement that Sikhs were an independent community:

> I do not keep the Hindu fast, nor the Muslim Ramadan;
> I serve Him alone who is my refuge.
> I serve the one Master who is also Allah.
> I have broken with the Hindu and the Muslim.
> I will not worship with the Hindu, nor like the Muslim go to Mecca,
> I shall serve Him and no other.
> I will not pray to idols nor say the Muslim prayer.
> I shall put my heart at the feet of the One Supreme Being;
> For we are neither Hindus nor Mussalmans.

Guru Arjun gave the Sikhs a place of pilgrimage of their own. They no longer had to go to Varanasi or Hardwar to wash away their sins in the Ganga, they would go to Amritsar and bathe in the pool surrounding the Harmandir. He gave them a scripture of their own, the Adi-granth which they could read and understand because it was in their mother tongue and did not need services of Brahmins to read out Sanskrit texts from the vedas or the upanishads which neither of them understood. With his execution in AD 1606 he also gave them their first martyr.

`With the death of Guru Arjun a new dimension was added to the Sikhs' separate identity. Arjun's son, the sixth Guru Hargovind (1595-1644), decided to arm his followers and proclaimed himself both spiritual and temporal head of the community *Mere peere da maalik.* Facing the Harmandir he built the Akal Takht (Throne of the Timeless God) where, instead of chanting hymns of peace, the congregation heard ballads extolling deeds of heroism, and instead of listening to sermons, they discussed plans of military campaigns. He asked his followers to make offerings of horses and arms and enrol as soldiers.

Thus far though the Sikhs had established a communal identity of their own, they continued to be regarded as the militant arm of Hinduism. This was reaffirmed in the martyrdom of ninth guru, Tegh Bahadur, known popularly as *Hind di chaadar* – Protector of India in AD 1678. The guru had appeared before the Mughal court as a representative of the Hindus of northern India to resist forcible conversion to Islam. His son, Guru Gobind Singh, described his father's martyrdom in the following words: 'To protect their right to wear their caste marks and sacred threads, did he in the dark age, perform the supreme sacrifice... He suffered martyrdom for the sake of his faith, he lost his head but revealed not his secret.'

Guru Gobind Singh (AD 1666-1708) brought about the final transformation of a pacificist Sikh community to a fraternity of the Khalsa Panth (Community of the Pure). From his writings it appears that he drew inspiration from martial deities like Goddesses Chandi, Sri and Bhagwati. At the same time he ordered his followers to wear their hair and beards unshorn, have one name 'Singh' and carry other symbols of the Khalsa including a *kirpan*. Thereafter a real Sikh was a Kesadhari Khalsa: he who did not subscribe to the Khalsa was either a Sahajdhari (slow adopters) or a Hindu believing in Sikhism.

For many generations the transition from Hindu to Kesadhari Khalsa remained an easy one as was evident in the almost overnight conversion of Lakshman Das, a Rajput of Poonch, and his assumption of the leadership of the Khalsa with the title Banda Bairagi or Banda Singh Bahadur (AD 1670-1710). It was under Banda's leadership that Khalsa armies won their earliest victories over the Mughals, Banda struck coins in the name of the Panth. The inscriptions on the coins were significant:

> Coins struck for the two worlds with the sword of Nanak
> And victory granted by the grace of Gobind Singh.

Banda and several hundred of his Khalsa soldiers were captured and executed in Mehrauli, near Delhi, in March 1710. Their blood created fertile soil for the sprouting of Sikh political power.

The relationship between the Hindus and the Khalsa remained extremely close as long as they were confronting the Mughals, Persian and Afghan invaders. Hindu youths coming to join the Khalsa simply let their hair and beards grow, accepted *pahul* (baptism) without breaking their family ties, it was during this period that the custom of bringing up one son as a Sikh grew amongst many Punjabi Hindu families. When Sikhs assumed power in Punjab under Maharaja Ranjit Singh (AD 1780-1839), Punjabi Hindus had even more reason to turn to the Khalsa. The Maharaja, though a devout Sikh, would also revere Brahmins, worship in Hindu temples and bathe in the Ganga. He made killing of cows a criminal offence punishable with death. Although he rebuilt the Harmandir in Amritsar in marble and gold leaf, when it came to disposing the Koh-i-Noor diamond his first preference was to gift it to the temple at Jaganathpuri.

The Sikh kingdom collapsed within ten years of Ranjit Singh's death. The British annexed Punjab in 1849. With an alien neutral party set up as arbiter of their destinies the relationships between Muslims, Hindus and Sikhs underwent a complete change. This had dramatic consequences on the close affinity between the Punjabi Hindus and Sikhs. They had been like one people, some bearded, others clean shaven but together forming a united front against Muslim onslaught or domination and equal partners during the years of triumphs under Ranjit Singh. With both the Muslim threat and the Sikh kingdom gone, external pressures that had kept them together disappeared. They had to redefine their mutual relationship. At the same time the British realized the advantages to them in keeping the Sikh identity separate from the Hindu. Assured of Sikh loyalty during the Mutiny of 1857 they rewarded Sikh princes and *zamindars* with grants of land and recruited Sikh soldiers in large numbers into their army provided they had taken the *pahul* and were orthodox Khalsa. An economic incentive was thus added to Sikh separatism.

The first blow to the Hindu-Sikh unity was struck by Arya Samaj. In 1877 Swami Dayanand Saraswati visited Punjab (oddly enough at the invitation of Sikh organizations) and opened a branch of the Samaj at Lahore. He launched his *shudhi* (purification) movement to bring breakaway Hindus including Sikhs back into the Hindu fold. Swamiji was intemperate in his speech; he described Guru Nanak as a *dambhi* (hypocrite) and the Granth Sahib as a book of secondary importance. The *Arya Samachar* published from Lahore lampooned Sikhism in the following verse:

Nanak Shah Fakeer ne naya chalaaya panth
Idhar udhar se jor kar likh mara ik granth;

Pehley cheley kar liye, pichhey badla bhes
Sir par saafa bandh kar, rakh leeney sab kes.

Sikh organizations retaliated with anger. Singh sabhas were set up in Amritsar and Lahore to counteract Arya Samaj propaganda. They had the blessings of the British government. A spate of books on Sikhism were published in Gurmukhi and English including the definitive six volumes by M.A. Macauliffe, *The Sikh Religion.* Amongst these was Kahan Singh's booklet, *Ham Hindu Nahi Hain*, 'We are not Hindus.'

The process of separatism was carried a step further by the Akali movement launched in the 1920s to wrest control of Sikh gurdwaras from hereditary *mahants* (priests) who had for generations been with non-kesadhari Sikhs or Hindus. The most significant outcome of the four years of intense Akali agitation in which the Hindus had supported the *mahants* was equivocally stated by Mahtab Singh in a speech in Punjab Legislative Council in April 1921. He said: 'I, for one, say that if the Sikhs do not wish to remain in the fold of Hinduism, why should the Hindus seek to force them to do so? What benefit can they obtain by keeping on unwilling people as partners in their community? Why not let them go?'

Some Hindu leaders tried to retrieve the situation. 'I look upon Sikhism as higher Hinduism,' said Raja Narindra Nath. Sir Gokul Chand Narang described them as 'the flesh of our flesh and the bone of our bones.' It was too late. The Sikh Gurdwara Act of 1925 which passed the control of Sikh temples to an elected body called the Shiromani Gurdwara Prabandhak Committee (SGPC) defined a Sikh as one who believed in the ten gurus and the Granth Sahib and did not believe in any other religion.

Separate electorates with reservations of seats gave the Sikhs their own constituencies from which they elected their own Sikh representatives. Reservations of proportions in civil and military services further ensured them that their privileges could only be enjoyed by the Khalsa. The British gave the Sikhs a vested interest in retaining the Khalsa identity distinct from the Hindu.

Relations between the two communities remained cordial, even intimate, as much as matrimonial alliances between members of the same caste living in urban areas continued as before. As Muslim pressure for a separate state mounted and Hindu-Muslim riots broke out in many parts of northern India, Hindus and Sikhs once again formed a united front the same way their forefathers had done to face Muslim invaders and tyrants. When Partition of the country became a reality both Hindus and Sikhs living in the part of western Punjab which went to Pakistan left their lands, hearths and homes and emigrated to India.

Partition of Punjab and Independence once again brought about a change in Hindu-Sikh relationship. Numbers had always been the chief problem of the Sikh community. At the time of Partition they formed no more than thirteen per cent of the population of the undivided Punjab and a bare one per cent of the population of India. Of the five million Sikhs, the prosperous half had their lands and homes in the part that went to Pakistan. They were the worst losers in the division of the country. This had serious impact on their fortunes as well as on their psyche. The two-and-a-half million that were expelled from Pakistan had been the richest peasantry of India owning large estates in the canal colonies. They changed places with the largely landless Muslim peasantry of east Punjab and had to take whatever little land that was made available to them as Muslims evacuee property.

Besides losing their land and properties Sikhs had to come to terms with secular India. Privileges they had enjoyed under the British rule by way of reservation of seats in legislatures and preferential treatment in the recruitment to the armed forces and civil services were abolished and they had to compete with other communities on the basis of merit.

Sikhs who had observed the Khalsa symbols of unshaven hair and beards only for the economic advantages that accrued began to give them up. Their numbers began to dwindle.

The abolition of separate electorate and the introduction of a joint one made the Sikhs, who were in a minority in all but a few districts of Indian Punjab, subservient to the Hindu majority. The Sikh community's point of view came to be expressed in purely communal organizations like the SGPC and local gurdwara committees.

However, since the Sikh migration was halted at certain points, for the first time in their history Sikhs came to form a majority of the population in some districts of Malwa. The deprivation combined with the fact that they had some regions where they predominated gave birth to the idea of an autonomous Sikh state. The sentiment was expressed in a single query: Hindus got Hindustan. Muslims got Pakistan. What did the Sikhs get out of Partition and Independence?

The notion of an autonomous Sikh state started taking shape with the announcement that boundaries of state would be drawn along linguistic lines. This was done for all the 14 major languages spoken in India except Punjabi. The Sikh rightly construed this as discrimination against the community and began to agitate for a Punjabi-speaking *suba*. Their task was made easier for them by the Punjabi Hindus who, sensing what the Sikhs were really after was a Sikh majority state, allowed themselves to be persuaded to declare to the census commissioners that their mother tongue was Hindi. The battle over language in effect became a confrontation between Punjabi Hindus and Punjabi Sikhs. The antagonism continued fitfully with passive resistance movements launched by the Akalis and fasts and threats of immolation by their leaders. Ultimately on the conclusion of the Indo-Pak War of 1965 in which the Sikh peasantry played a notable role helping Indian troops on the front line, a commission was appointed to demarcate Punjabi speaking areas from the Hindi-speaking. Thus, in 1966 Punjab was split into three states: Haryana, Himachal and Punjabi-speaking Punjab in which Sikhs formed about 60 per cent of the population.

The story of the new Indian Punjab since its inception has been one of political instability against the background of spectacular advances made in agriculture. On the political front, governments came and went – sometimes of the Congress, at others of Akalis allied with the BJP interspersed with president's rule. At the same time Sikh peasants took to modernizing their farming methods by using tractors, introducing new varieties of hybrid seeds developed in the Ludhiana Agricultural University, using fertilizers, insecticides and harvesters. The yield per acre was doubled and then trebled. The Green Revolution in wheat was followed by similar increase in the production of rice and sugarcane. There were not enough flour, rice or sugar mills in the state to process the produce.

Prosperity brought its own problems. At harvest time labourers from UP and Bihar began to come in thousands to Punjab to work as farm-hands on daily wages. Many decided to settle there and were enrolled on the voters lists. At the same time large number of Sikhs began to migrate to Western countries. Thus, the proportion of Sikhs began to decline. The Akali party also discovered to its dismay that although it had been the chief instrument in getting the suba, when it came to wielding power it was more often than not that the Congress party won at the polls and grasped the sceptre. A sense of disillusionment crept in.

By the middle of the 1970s the Green Revolution had reached a plateau state with bumper harvests levelling out. At the same time the already small land-holdings became even smaller as families multiplied. Employment opportunities abroad were seriously curtailed by stringent visa regulations imposed by foreign governments. This, combined with the absence of industries in the state, resulted in a rapid and alarming increase in the number of educated unemployed.

Thus, volatile human material was created for politicians to exploit.

In April 1973 the Akalis took another step which they thought would ensure Sikh hegemony in Punjab's affairs. This was the passing of the Anandpur Sahib Resolution. In this controversial resolution (at least three different versions are in circulation) the Sikhs were described as a separate nation. It also demanded greater autonomy for the state, readjustment of the states' boundaries including Punjabi-speaking areas which had been given to Himachal, Haryana and Rajasthan.

Not much notice was taken of the Anandpur Sahib Resolution at the time it was passed and later ratified by the Akali Dal. Even during the time the Akalis formed governments in Punjab, they took scant notice of it. However, it was to the credit of the Akali party that when Mrs Gandhi declared the state of Emergency on 26 June 1975, the Akalis not only opposed it but continued to agitate against it by sending batches of volunteers to offer themselves for arrest. Most Akali leaders spent the Emergency years in jail. It paid them handsome dividends. In the elections that followed the lifting of the Emergency, the Akalis carried the electorate with them and in alliance with the Janata formed a government on 27 March 1977 under the chief ministership of Prakash Singh Badal.

The Akali-Janata government lasted barely two years. As the Janata government at the centre fell and Mrs Gandhi returned as prime minister, she dissolved the states' legislatures including that of Punjab and called for new elections. The Congress party routed the Akali-Janata combine and Darbara Singh was elected chief minister.

The Congress party government under Darbara Singh proved disastrous for the state. For one, Darbara Singh and his predecessor Giani Zail Singh who had been inducted into the central cabinet as home minister, were forever throwing spanners in each other's works. For another, Akalis, now out of power and with little prospect of regaining it through the electoral process, decided to destabilize the Congress government through agitation. They hauled the Anandpur Sahib Resolution out of the archives and proclaimed it as a charter of Sikh demands. To this they tagged another 45 ranging from the substantial ones like readjustment of the state's boundaries and a fairer allocation of waters of Rivers Sutlej and Beas to which it was the only riparian state, to the utterly trivial ones like renaming a train as the Golden Temple Express and banning sale of cigarettes, liquor and meat in the vicinity of the Golden Temple. They followed it up with a series of agitations: *nahar roko* (blocking the canal meant to link Punjab's river waters with the Yamuna), *rasta roko* (block road traffic), *kam roko* (stop work). And finally declared a *dharamyudh* (righteous war) from Amritsar against the government by sending over a thousand volunteers a day to court arrest.

Alongside this passive resistance movement a parallel Sikh fundamentalist movement began to build up under the leadership of Jarnail Singh Bhindranwale (1947-84). It had begun with the confrontation between orthodox Khalsa and Nirankaris in Amritsar on 13 April 1978 in which 13 lives were lost, mainly of Bhindranwale's followers. The Nirankaris put on trial were acquitted by a judge who found that they had acted in self-defence. Jarnail Singh Bhindranwale swore vengeance. The Akalis lent their support to him. From the Akal Takht the Nirankaris were proclaimed as enemies of the Khalsa Panth. On 24 April 1980, Baba Gurbachan Singh, the Nirankari guru, was assassinated in Delhi by Bhindranwale followers. This was followed by the killings of many Nirankaris in different parts of Punjab. Nevertheless, Bhindranwale was allowed to go about freely, toured Bombay and Delhi and when arrested was let off. He became a formidable force and gathered round him groups of terrorists mainly from unemployed youths belonging to the All India Sikh Students Federation. From slaying Nirankaris, terrorists expanded their 'hit lists' to include Nirankari sympathizers, dissident Akalis and Congress party members.

Their chief target was the Hindu-owned Jullundur based chain of papers. On 9 September 1981, Lala Jagat Narain, chief editor of *Punjab Kesari,* was shot dead. A year later Jagat Narain's son, Ramesh Chander, fell to their bullets. Amongst those killed were H.S. Manchanda, president of the Delhi Gurdwara Prabandhak Committee, DIG of Police A.S. Atwal, Dr V.N. Tiwari, nominated member of parliament and Gyani Pratap Singh, a retired priest. Many Hindu temples were desecrated and innocent Hindu and Sikhs killed in cold blood. It was obvious that the terrorists' ranks had been infiltrated by Pakistani agents, smugglers, Naxalites and common dacoits. The police were rarely able to identify or arrest the culprits. Its only method of dealing with the menace was to organize fake encounters and kill anyone they supported. And while the *morcha* continued, no Akali leader condemned these senseless killings in the language they deserved to be condemned nor had the courage to denounce Bhindranwale. The administration was totally paralysed. Meanwhile many meetings took place between Akali leaders and government representatives – issues were narrowed down and on at least two occasions agreement was within easy grasp when the talks had to be called off. It is difficult to say who was at fault, the Akalis or the government. Undoubtedly both.

When Bhindranwale sensed that the government had at long last decided to arrest him he first took shelter in the Golden Temple, then occupied and fortified portions of the Akal Takht. In full view of hundreds of armed constables, sophisticated arms including light machine guns and hand grenades were smuggled in. Killings which had so far been carried out beyond the precincts of the temple spread to the sacred precincts as rival gangs slew members of the other.

By the spring of 1984 it was clear that the day of reckoning between the authorities and Bhindranwale could not be put off for long. Akali leaders out of fear were unwilling or unable to order Bhindranwale out of the temple complex. The administration could not make up its mind about how and when to act. Mrs Gandhi's advisers were unable to arrive at any settlement with Akalis and on a number of occasions when virtually all points of dispute had been resolved, they withdrew from their commitments, fearing that an agreement with the Akalis might be construed as yielding to pressure and might have adverse reaction on the numerically much larger Hindu vote in northern India. There were times when a force of commandos in plain clothes would have easily overpowered Bhindranwale and his men, who did not exceed a couple of hundred men spread out over the temple complex, and taken them alive or dead. Nor was it considered feasible to occupy the Guru ka Langar by force, or deprive Bhindranwale and his men of food and fuel and force them out of their entrenchment to come out and fight. On the contrary, the situation was allowed to develop to an explosive point and the worst possible time was chosen for action. On 3 June 1984 was the anniversary of the martyrdom of Guru Arjun Dev. Thousands of pilgrims who had come from neighbouring villages were staying in the temple Sarai and the Parikrama. On 1 June, the army took over the state, cut off all communications with the outside world and imposed curfew in the city of Amritsar. Sporadic exchange of fire began on 1 June and continued for the next three days. On the evening of 5 June, the army entered the temple complex with tanks and armoured personnel carrier and blasted the Akal Takht. No one will ever know the final figure of casualties except that it was well over a thousand (three times more than Jallianwala Bagh in 1919) and hundreds of innocent men, women and children were killed. The Akal Takht including some priceless relics was in shambles. The temple archives which contained hundreds of handwritten copies of Granth Sahib and scores of *Hukumnamas* bearing signatures of the gurus went up in flames. Contrary to the government's contention that the Harmandir had been untouched, scores of bullet marks were later found piercing its marble and wooden windows. The premises were subjected to extensive looting. Gurdwara *golaks* (money-pitchers) were emptied. Cash and office equipment in the SGPC and Akali Dal offices were taken. To destroy all evidences, entire buildings with all their records were set on fire.

The most damning judgement of Operation Bluestar is that the government did not foresee what the reaction of the Sikh community numbering 14 million would be to the storming of their holiest of holy shrines. The vast majority of Sikhs had no sympathy for Bhindranwale and were indeed nauseated by his venomous utterances and the senseless killings by his gun-men. Some who had submitted to Akali politics were disillusioned by their leaders lack of foresight. Most had no interest in politics of any sort. And it was they who felt that the government had used Bhindranwale as an excuse to give the entire Sikh community a bloody punch in their nose.

With the strict censorship imposed in Punjab, all we know of Operation Bluestar is the army-cum-government version of the action. It may be quite some time before we get to know the other side of the story. It is therefore only fair that readers should have some idea of what people who were present and witnessed the entire episode have to say. Of the hundreds of accounts received by me – with forgivable exaggerations by people who went through the ordeal – I have chosen one by Bhan Singh, secretary of the Akali Dal because it is a factual narration of incidents that took place. This is what he has to say:

'On the morning of 1 June 1984, CRPF began to fire on the Golden Temple from different directions. The firing continued all day. As a result of this firing one Kulwant Singh was killed in Baba Atal Gurdwara and five men were killed in the Akal Takht. The firing was reckless and 32 bullet marks were seen on the walls of the Harmandir.

'On 3 June, curfew was imposed on the entire state; all manner of traffic was stopped and communication including telephones were cut off. Sunday, 3 June was the anniversary of the martyrdom of Guru Arjun. Because of the relaxation in the curfew pilgrims had been able to enter the Parikrama. A large number of them slept the night in the Parikrama. So did many *sevadars*, *paathis* (scripture readers) and the devout who voluntarily clean temple premises at night. Volunteers numbering between 1800 to 1900 who had come to participate in the *dharamyudh morcha* to offer themselves for arrest were in Teja Singh Samundari Hall and Guru Ram Das Niwas. Amongst them were 1300 Akali workers under the leadership of Jathedar Nacchattar Singh including 200 women and 18 children.

'On the morning of 4 June at 4.40 a.m. army cannons and machine-guns began to fire. There was no kind of notice or warning given. The firing went on all day into the night. I spent the night in my office in Teja Singh Samundari Hall. Most of the shells fell on the Akal Takht, Baba Atal, the Water Tower, Guru Nanak Niwas, Guru Ram Das Langar, and buildings behind the Akal Takht. Firing continued till five o'clock of the evening of 5 June. At 5.15 p.m. two Sikhs came from the Baghwali Gali which runs behind Guru Ram Das Niwas with the message that Sardar Abhashi Singh was wanted outside by Sardar Apar Singh Bajwa, DSP with the news that the army would stop firing from 4 to 5.30 p.m., so that anyone who wanted to come out could do so. I and Abhashi Singh conveyed the information to Sant Longowal and Sardar Gurucharan Singh Tohra. They asked me, S. Balwant Singh Ramoowalia and Abhashi Singh to go out and persuade the DSP to extend the time by an hour so that women, children and other helpless people could get out. However, while we were still at the *gali*, the firing was resumed with even greater intensity. During the interval about 40 to 50 armed Sikhs came from the Parikrama to Guru Ram Das Niwas, took positions on the rooftop and began to return the army's fire. With this the army bombardment came to be directed towards Guru Ram Das Niwas, Teja Singh Samundari Hall and rooms of the Dharam Prachar Committee. We sat down in the middle room of Teja Singh Samundari Hall while Sant Longowal and Tohra along with ten Sikhs went into the president's room. We spent the entire night awake because of the firing.

'On the morning of 6 June, the army came inside Guru Ram Das Niwas and entered Teja Singh Samundari Hall. Sant Longowal, Tohra, Bibi Amarjit Kaur and other Sikhs with them were taken into custody by the jawans led by two officers and escorted away. We followed them from Teja Singh Samundari Hall towards Ram Das Niwas. In this time about 200 to 250 Sikhs collected, of which many sat down in the courtyard of the *niwas.* From the upper storey of the *niwas* a grenade fell on them. Jatheder Bagga Singh, a soldier and some Sikhs were killed. Nacchattar Singh's leg was blown off. He did not receive medical attention and succumbed to his injuries after four hours. When the grenade fell it was still somewhat dark. Soldiers lost their temper and began to fire wildly killing between 30 to 35 people including women, children and aged people. Amongst the many who were injured were committee employees, Raj Singh, Dayal Singh and Gurubachan Singh. The injured men came to me and asked for medical help. I spoke to a *subedar* who sent a soldier to escort me to his major. When I got to the major I saw about 35 or 36 young Sikhs lined up with their hands raised above their heads and the major was about to order them to be shot. When I asked him for medical help he got into a rage, tore my turban off my head and ordered his men to shoot me. I turned back and fled jumping over bodies of the dead and injured and saved my life by crawling along the walls. I got to the room where Tohra and Sant Longowal were sitting and told them of what I had seen. S. Karnail Singh Nag who had followed me also narrated what he had seen as well as the killing of 35 to 36 young Sikhs by cannon fire. All these youngmen were villagers of which about 20 to 21 wore long *darhi* and others were *mona.* All of them had been hauled out of the Guru Ram Das Sarai. This incident took place about 8.30 p.m.

'We had nothing to eat or drink the day earlier. This day also we went hungry and thirsty. At about 4 o'clock, Tohra, Sant Longowal and their companions were taken out. People were crying for water. Some slaked their thirst with dirty water which had run down the damaged water tank and was mixed with blood and dirt of the courtyard. Of them nearly 120 were injured. There was no Red Cross or medical aid of any kind available for them. At 7 o'clock they began to remove the corpses and by 9 we were taken to military camps. I reached there at 9.30. I and my companions were released on 23 June 1984.'

Signed
BHAN SINGH
23 June 1984

Akali Dal: The Enemy Within

AMARJIT KAUR

The phenomenon of Khalistan has been there ever since the partition of this subcontinent into India and Pakistan. At the time of Independence, or just before, there was a significant number of people among the young Akali workers and junior leadership who actually thought that the time for a 'Sikh state' had come since the country was being divided. The British had, in fact, encouraged this line of thinking.

Fortunately, the older generation of Sikh leaders: the Akalis led by Master Tara Singh, the feudal elements led by the former rulers of the states of Patiala, Kapurthala, Jind, Faridkot and Nabha, and the old Sardari clique led by people like Sardar Baldev Singh, Raja Harinder Singh and Sardar Hukam Singh, in their wisdom, decided not to fall in with the designs of the British rulers and to cast their lot with India.

The younger elements within the Akali Dal who were for a separate Sikh state might have been defeated at that point in history; but, they were not deterred from working for this goal.

Unfortunately, the older leadership within the Akali Dal inadvertently played into the hands of the fundamentalists and the separatists amongst the younger leadership when they began to proclaim that Sikh politics could not be separated from the Sikh religion since this was a fact of life proclaimed by the gurus.

There were two simple reasons why no Sikh challenged this concept created so conveniently by the Akali Dal. The common man amongst the Sikhs was not really bothered about such issues; he was too busy building a life for himself. Secondly, there was an acute lack of knowledge of Sikh history and scriptures amongst the Sikh masses. Consequently, the Akali Dal could feed their Sikh followers anything and they would accept it as the gospel truth.

Over the years as the younger generation began to replace the older, fundamentalism began to raise its ugly head and religion and politics began to be mixed even more, the distant glimmer of a Sikh-dominated state began to appear – and conflicts began between the moderate and those who imagined this distant glimmer – the first step towards a Sikh state, or as it is now called, Khalistan.

It is essential to understand the fact that the older generation of Akali leaders believed that the only way to create a mass base amongst the Sikh community was to appeal to the religious sentiments of the Sikhs. They wanted to appear as the only guardians of the Sikh faith. And as such, the bogey of Hindu communalism and domination became a convenient tool. Their eventual aim was to become the only spokesman of the Sikhs. The interpretation of religion became their prerogative and the existing administrative Sikh body of the SGPC became their lever, as well as their financier for all their future political activities.

The younger leadership which took over was more or less composed of uneducated *jathedars* such as Gurcharan Singh Tohra, Talwandi, etc. They began to use the SGPC as a treasury to render possible their dreams of an eventual Sikh majority state. This was how the Punjabi *suba* movement came into being. The issue of language – Punjabi in the Gurmukhi script – was only a pretext then, as is the Anandpur Sahib Resolution today, towards this end.

The educated Akali leadership such as Prakash Singh Badal, Justice Gurnam Singh and Lachman Singh Gill believed that they could politically outmanoeuvre their uneducated colleagues and take over the leadership of the Akalis.

Consequently, these educated leaders allowed communalism to cast a shadow over their party's political concepts. Their reasoning: their existence was dependent on Sikh votes and such votes could only come their way through religious exploitation.

These leaders felt that since the Akali Dal could never come to power in Punjab before 1966 and since the state was not Sikh-dominated, the Punjabi suba movement had to be started.

However, even after obtaining the Punjabi suba in 1966, their political fortunes did not improve significantly. The dominance of the Sikh community was confined to only two per cent, which they realized was insufficient to keep them in power because of the inherent conflicts within the party itself.

Whenever they did come to power, they ended up breaking into two or three factions; sometimes the divide occurred between the educated and the uneducated sections. Moreover, their government would always fall before the full five-year term only to be succeeded in a by-election by the Congress party.

Another cause for the growing frustration of the Akalis was the fact that the Sikh community at large did not fall for their ploy that they were the only spokesmen of their community, or for that matter that the Sikh *panth* was in danger.

Gradually, santdom began to dominate Punjabi politics. Fateh Singh then, Bhindranwale now. All these uneducated *jathedars* who took over the command of Akali leadership knew the words of the scriptures but not their spirit.

After the division of PEPSU into three States – which harmed the Punjabis because Punjab had shrunk – inter-party factions emerged, as mentioned earlier. Following this there was a rift between the Jats and the Khatris: Master Tara Singh was a Khatri. The Jat Akalis followed the others to a point when they were able to, and began to dominate Akali politics. This took place in 1962 with the emergence of Fateh Singh.

The Jats succeeded in ousting the Khatris; the conflict still exists, though with a kind of split between the urban and the rural Sikhs. Significantly, once the Jats took over the Akali leadership, conflicts within the Jats arose. Each group began to espouse demands which increased until they came to the point of Khalistan.

The opposition has mentioned the fact that Bhindranwale was an election agent or was supported by one or two Congress(I) MPs and that he was a plant of Congress(I). The opposition blames the Congress(I) for the emergence of Bhindranwale; but I would like to know who invited Bhindranwale into Guru Nanak Niwas and into the premises of the Golden Temple. The SGPC president, Mr Tohra and the moderate leadership of the Akalis helped Bhindranwale; otherwise nobody can live in the premises of the Golden Temple without the permission of the SGPC president. After all, Bhindranwale did not just walk in.

I feel that they used Bhindranwale for their own political reasons against the government. They built up Bhindranwale not realizing that, much later, he would become a Frankenstein. But towards the end, the Akalis became helpless. The Frankenstein they had created, under the garb of their *dharamyudh* for their own political ends, was to eventually compete with them. And ultimately, to swallow them.

The Akali Dal and its so-called moderate leadership were constantly tripping over their own big feet in their attempt to justify their political stunts in their endeavour to establish themselves after their electoral defeat in 1980. They became helpless. Towards the end, their agitation had failed. To begin with, the Akalis tried an agitation in Kapoori village in Patiala district over the water issue. The agitation failed because none of the people of the area supported the Kapoori agitation.

Later, when Bhindranwale shifted into the Guru Nanak Niwas, Sant Harchand Singh Longowal also moved into the Golden Temple. Competition began between the two: who was going to be the leader of the *morcha*. The first issue was taken up by the moderate Akalis and Sant Bhindranwale. One of the main issues was the release of Tara Singh and Bhai Amreek Singh.

Bhindranwale actually came into prominence after his arrest in Mehta Chowk in 1981; but he had already emerged from the background after the clash between the Nirankaris and Sikhs on 13 April 1978 when several of Bhindranwale's followers were killed. Bhindranwale, who had been in the background until then, at this stage joined hands with other Sikh sants against the government.

The Akalis were in power then but Mr Tohra at this point decided to support Bhindranwale in order to embarrass Mr Badal. In fact, the Punjab government even passed a rule that no Nirankari gathering could take place in Punjab.

At the time of Bhindranwale's arrest in Mehta Chowk, the Akalis supported him wholeheartedly, both with emotional speeches and even in their demands. They had actually said that Bhindranwale's life was in danger and that the government was either trying to assassinate him or to have him assassinated. All this shows that they started protecting him, or fighting for him. They asked for his unconditional release in the first point of the revised list of the 15 demands given to the government in October 1981.

Meanwhile, Bhindranwale had begun his fiery speeches and used to say openly that he would weigh the person in gold who would fetch him the Nirankari chief, Baba Gurbachan Singh's head.

The government could have arrested him at that stage but it required somebody saying that they had proof. The government did not want to take the risk, as they had to release him, earlier, for the lack of any legal proof.

Everybody was frightened because they felt that if they did give any evidence against Bhindranwale or against any of his men, they and their entire families would be killed.

Bhindranwale had put fear into the people because innocent people were being killed and any officer who went against his wishes was killed. It is but natural that if a person who is told that his life would be in danger if he did not give up his job, would eventually give up his job. They eliminated, one by one, all the witnesses in the Nirankari case.

There were other occasions when Bhindranwale could have been arrested, or when the government was planning to arrest him. But Bhindranwale had planted his own people in government offices, in the police, in the intelligence agencies. He had a big network. He had all these ex-army officers behind him – they plotted and planned for him. They had responded to the call which Bhindranwale had given.

He had actually started by involving the Sikh students and the All India Sikh Students Federation by demanding the release of its president, Bhai Amreek Singh. The AISSF had already been misused by him.

There were other more complex reasons why Bhindranwale could not have been stopped earlier. Political reasons, shall we say. A cordial relationship between the then home minister and the chief minister might have avoided many mistakes. Sardar Darbara Singh blamed all his misdeeds on the home minister. He kept saying: 'I wanted to do this but he stopped me.' When Mr Atwal was murdered, Mr Darbara Singh wanted to enter the Golden Temple but he was, he said, stopped by Giani Zail Singh who was then the home minister.

Why should Darbara Singh as chief minister have to blame anybody else? Every chief minister has his opponents within his party. His capability, his statesmanship, his ability as an administrator – all these qualities ought to help him overcome these problems.

Gianiji, as chief minister, faced all these problems. Darbara Singh used to oppose him at every step; even Sardar Swaran Singh, G.S. Dhillon and the other Sikh leadership in the Congress used to oppose him. Giani Zail Singh was alone, but, he was able to manage well on his own. Which chief minister does not face problems within his party? It is up to him to manage.

Had it not been for Sardar Darbara Singh's mishandling of the situation, president's rule need not have been imposed.

I am quite convinced that the government was not aware of the extent to which Bhindranwale and his men were armed. I was told by some people in the press that when they went to the Golden Temple, interviews were taped and they were warned from saying anything other than what was taped. Some were even told what to write.

Nor could there have been any government informer. If these people found anyone doing so they would shoot them and throw their bodies into the drains. Nobody dared open his mouth. Bhindranwale had his own men spying on people inside the Golden Temple.

There is also another reason why the government did not really know what was going on inside the Golden temple. During the Janata regime, when Morarji Desai was the prime minister, the intelligence agencies received a great setback. Some of the secrets and names of informers are only supposed to be known to the prime minister. During this time, this information was leaked out. It is the reason why the intelligence feedback on terrorist activity was hopeless.

Perhaps, one of the reasons why the army was rather suddenly sent into the Golden Temple – I say suddenly because all along, the government was reluctant to send in the army – was the threat to kill all Congress(I) MPs and MLAs on 5 June and their plan to begin mass killing of Hindus in villages.

In my district, Balbera in Patiala four or five *arthyas* were killed hardly a fortnight before the army action; the mass killings had already started. In Model Town an architect, a doctor and other innocent Hindus were being killed. They aimed to kill more. Actually, they wanted to start a civil war between the Hindus and the Sikhs.

They were killing the Sikhs who had vocally opposed Bhindranwale and the idea of Khalistan.

During my mass contact programme in Patiala district in May 1984, we faced so many angry people. The Patiala gurdwara, Dukhanwaran, was coming up as a sub-centre of the terrorist movement. Harvinder Singh Khalsa was camping in our district and coordinating the activities from there. People in my constituency refused to talk to me. Why are you not taking any action, they asked? Gurdwaras are no longer gurdwaras if terrorists were hiding there, they told me. How many more innocent people will be killed?

These activities must have prompted the army action. Otherwise, the army might have been better prepared. The army had thought that the operation would last only one hour: they would surround Harmandir Sahib and ask the people inside to surrender and the latter would come out. And it would all be over.

Had the extremists done so, all this would have been avoided. But people inside the Golden Temple began to fire in return. Bhindranwale went into the Akal Takht because he realized that the government would not enter Harmandir Sahib. Bhindranwale took full advantage of the fact that Sikh feelings would be hurt if anything happened to the Akal Takht. As a Sikh, I reacted strongly... but it had all become too much.

When Bhindranwale shifted into the Akal Takht, Sikhs should have openly criticized his move. Sikhs should have also told the SGPC president and the other Akali leaders who had encouraged all this to bring Bhindranwale out of the Akal Takht. They should have strongly objected to the role of the Akalis.

I did at that time appeal to the Sikhs to come out and strongly oppose Bhindranwale's moving into the Akal Takht. In fact, I said that Bhindranwale should be asked to leave the Golden Temple. Why did he not come out and fight if he was so brave? If he was innocent why did he not come out and prove his innocence? Why was he taking shelter in the premises of the Golden Temple and encouraging smugglers, anti-social and anti-national elements? Why was he collecting arms through smugglers, collecting money, encouraging people to loot and share the booty with them? For a saint to preach violence is something new!

He definitely had links with the Pakistanis and Americans. After all, he had links with Ganga Singh Dhillon and Jagjit Singh Chauhan. I was told many years ago by people who had visited Canada that the Sikhs living in that country had already decided to have a Khalistan in Punjab.

I would like to know how people who have left India and have become American or Canadian citizens can dictate terms to us. They are no longer Indians. They have no business to act as foreign agents in our homeland.We received Khalistan currency notes a few months ago and pamphlets about how the Sikhs were being discriminated against. Many Sikhs had, in fact, stated that they were being discriminated against and when there was no other way for them to enter other countries they began to use the word, 'political asylum.' This was the only way to migrate and get jobs in those countries. By doing this they disgraced our community and our country.

Khalistan has always been in the minds of some people. Even the moderates did not openly condemn the killings. Why did the Akalis not strongly condemn Bhindranwale's actions? If they disagreed with the killings, they should have done so openly. If, in fact, Tohra disagreed with their actions he should have asked them to leave the precincts of the Golden Temple.

Tohra, in fact, played his own political game. He made Bhindranwale fight against moderates like Sant Longowal and

Badal for his own political gains. He played one against the other.

Moreover, if Bhindranwale had any differences with Tohra, the latter would take the help of Sant Longowal and Badal. If on the other hand Tohra disagreed with Badal and Sant Longowal, he would take shelter with Bhindranwale. Tohra played the most devious game by using both the moderates and the extremists for his own political ends.

Ever since Tohra took up the SGPC presidentship, he has concentrated on bringing politics into the gurdwaras instead of preaching the Sikh religion from there. He involved the Sikh religion with politics to such an extent that religion was totally forgotten during his tenure. I would also like to stress again at this point that the moderates, including Badal, also want Khalistan. What after all is the Anandpur Sahib Resolution? Indirectly, they were asking for a separate nation. Which government would accept such a resolution? During the talks, the Akalis never forgot the Anandpur Sahib Resolution; they always brought up the subject. The moderates would not admit the fact that they were really heading towards the implementation of the Anandpur Sahib Resolution, but their actions indicated this. When they knew that what Bhindranwale was projecting was nothing else but Khalistan – in his tapes he made rather devastating speeches – they had no reason not to disown him.

To begin with, the Akalis did not know exactly what they wanted. Each time they came to the talks which took place many times, they would bring up a new demand. Firstly, they came up with the religious demands, later the other demands. Mrs Gandhi agreed to the religious demands, and she even announced this.

But these religious demands could not be implemented because the Akalis began to disagree. They went into details such as how many inches the *kirpans* allowed on Indian Airlines flights should be, how many hours the Gurbani should be relayed from Harmandir Sahib.

Perhaps, they did not want these demands to be implemented because they were either afraid of Bhindranwale or of each other. When contacted individually, the Akali leaders would agree, but collectively, they would disagree. Moreover, every time secret talks were to be held, the information managed to be leaked out to the Akalis or to Bhindranwale and an agreement became impossible, with each member being wary of the other, or forewarned, as the case might be.

Perhaps, all these prevarications were delaying tactics. Article 25 was never there in the beginning. But it suddenly cropped up.

They wanted to eliminate the word Hindu. They used to come up with all these foolish things, without going into details of the real issues involved. For instance, whether Article 25 would be useful or harmful to the Sikhs in the long run. The government even said that retired judges could look into the matter.

But the Akalis continued to shift their stand. They would agree on something during the talks and then go back and change their minds. During the last few talks, the extremists had taken complete hold of the situation. Even the Akalis had begun to feel that things had gone beyond their control and that even they were now controlled by the extremists. The moderates did not realize until it was too late. In fact, they informed the prime minister that they were helpless and could no longer do anything about the extremists. They even asked for government protection because they felt that their lives were in danger. Longowal was sending frantic messages to the government to save him.

Whenever they agreed on something or talks were about to take place a murder of a prominent person would disrupt the talks. For instance, when talks were about to take place, Professor Tiwari a member of the Rajya Sabha was killed. The talks were postponed.

Again later, when the atmosphere for talks was created after the moderate Sikhs were released from prison, where they were taken after they had burned copies of Article 25 of the constitution, Lala Jagat Narain's son, Ramesh Chander, was murdered. Again, the talks were postponed.

Obviously, they were not interested in resolving matters. The government even invited the opposition for the tripartite talks and told them that they should try and get the Akalis to agree. The opposition was told that they should know what was happening. The Akalis walked out of the tripartite talks. There was a discussion in the Rajya Sabha when the talks were on – Badal was sitting in the gallery then – and the opposition leaders involved in the tripartite talks said that they could not understand why the Akalis had walked out of the talks when everything had been finalized. The opposition, in fact, requested the Akalis to come back to the talks in the interest of the state and the nation.

By 1983, General Shabeg Singh, other retired army officers and IAS officers or those who were to resign later, were guiding Bhindranwale. The Sikhs in Canada, UK and the USA also played their role bv remote control – plotting and planning.

POLITICS AND RELIGION

We must now amend the Sikh Gurdwara Act of 1925. An unambiguous clause which clearly states that elected members, office-bearers and employees of the SGPC cannot under any circumstances hold a political post, should be incorporated into the act. Any employee who wants to indulge in politics must resign his SGPC position first. In fact, the funds and the working of the SGPC should be audited annually by the government and it should also be opened to public scrutiny. These findings could even be published in the form of a gazette during the budget period.

Moreover, if a majority of the Sikhs express a desire to administer their gurdwaras themselves, this act could be repealed. The government should definitely introduce a law which prohibits temples of all faiths from being used by anti-social or anti-national elements, or as storehouses for lethal weapons, except those declared to be of historical value by the government.

Politics and religion should be completely separated. The Hindus actually began to feel claustrophobic after the *hukumnama* was issued in 1978 against the Nirankaris. Hindus began to feel that if it is the Nirankaris today, tomorrow it will be them. All the *maths* within the community: the Radhasoamis, Udasis, Namdharis, Nirmalas, began to worry about the fact that political *hukumnamas* could be handed out against them as well. We Sikhs who belong to the Congress party began to feel that, in future they could issue the *hukumnama* at will and even command us to join the Akali party.

The liberal Sikh was also outraged. After all, there can be a few Nirankaris in each family. They cannot tell us not to mix with our brothers if they become Nirankaris.

Immediately after this *hukumnama* was issued, I wrote an article denouncing the *hukumnama*: I wanted to create a controversy in the universities about this. I had said that these were political *hukumnamas* which did not have any religious meanings. At the same time, Tohra had written to the then railways minister, Mr Madhu Dandavate, to name the Flying Mail the Golden Temple Express. I objected to this. 1 even wrote a letter to Mr Dandavate to warn him that this kind of thing would create problems between the Hindus and the Sikhs. The Akalis would want the *kirtan* to be relayed and smoking prohibited. They really wanted a 'gurdwara-on-wheels.'

What is now worrying is the Hindu-Sikh divide. After the army action many Sikhs withdrew into their shells. Every village in Punjab has its hard core Akalis. The small gurdwaras are being used for political purposes; they have become the headquarters in each village for the hard core Akalis who are supported by the well-to-do Jat farmers. These are the people who prevent the Harijans from voting during elections. They bully the village into submission. But fortunately it does not always work.

A positive sign today is the fact that the farmers are now beginning to show that they are more concerned about their economic problems than the religious ones. While all the arrests were taking place over the *kar seva* of the Akal Takht, the farmers in my district held big demonstrations outside the district collector's house. These farmers were demanding more short-term loans, and a reduction in the power tariff. They did not mention any religious demands!

The Kheti Bari Union which later merged with the Bharatiya Kisan Union is becoming a major force in Punjab and none of the office bearers are allowed to be affiliated with any political party. These farmers are also aware of the fact that the Akalis exploited them.

It will take some time to remove the feelings of mistrust welling up between the Hindus and Sikhs. The division between the two communities is there. But I cannot understand why Sikhs are hesitant to face facts. We knew what was happening inside the Golden Temple: it had become a fortress and was no longer a gurdwara. Yet, there was this reluctance on the part of many Sikhs, especially after the army action, to be objective.

There seems to be a mental block, particularly amongst the intelligentsia. The intellectuals should know where things went wrong. Most of them however have been carried away emotionally; they do not want to listen to reason, to believe what is true.

I am in the process of trying to understand this closed-door attitude of the Sikh intelligentsia after the army action. The Sikh intellectual tends to see Hindu communalism behind every bush. He aggravates this feeling of insecurity by immersing himself even further in ritualistic dogmas, adhering to the letter rather than the spirit of the law. He is deliberately throwing himself backwards in time to the seventeenth century just at the moment when we are on the threshold of the twenty-first century.

Can the intellectuals deny the fact that when any brave and democratic Sikh stood up to question the barbaric acts, duly sanctioned by the author of the 'hit lists' living in the safety of Akal Takht, he was called a traitor to the community and shot dead. The shooting of the Sikhs by this fanatic was part of a design to subvert the inherent courage of the Sikh community as a whole and to reduce us to a community of cowards in subjugation to this fanatic.

The 'hit list' stopped the thought-process in the minds of many Sikh intellectuals. It conjured up the picture of the menacing shape of the loaded Stengun which stopped dead in its tracks any resistance to what the terrorists had set out to achieve.

Many Sikh intellectuals may have seen the signs of communalism emerging in the Sikh community; but they conveniently looked the other way – they preferred to take shelter under the argument that Akali demands were Punjabi demands and the only solution possible was for the government to surrender to the *dharamyudh* of the Akali Dal.

A large number of Sikh intellectuals may have spoken out against terrorism in Punjab, but they did so from the safety of their homes and offices. Why did they not go alone or in a *sangat* of tens, hundreds, thousands to the Akal Takht to demand that Bhindranwale and his murdering henchmen vacate their sacriligious occupation of our most sacred gurdwara. We Sikhs should have had the courage to solve this problem ourselves. I am also as guilty as the next Sikh because I was quite content to let the government cleanse my home. I should set my own house in order.

Amarinder Singh resigned from the Congress(I) after the army action because he had no alternative. His family had links with the sixth guru Hargobind Rai who built the Akal Takht.

The sixth guru had blessed the Patiala family: he had said: *Tera ghar so mera aas hai.* It was because of this personal link that Amarinder Singh had to resign.

Amarinder had said earlier that if the army entered the Golden Temple, he would have to leave. But nobody knew that the army was going to enter the temple's premises.

The Akali Dal and the SGPC have, by not throwing out Bhindranwale from the premises of the Golden Temple, lost the right to speak for and on behalf of the Sikhs. The Sikh community as a whole expects that the head priests at least should be above the fear of man. But these head priests became soundless wonders.

And for them to now insist that the *kar seva* should only be done under their guidance is a bit hypocritical, to say the least. A big thing is being made of the Sikh *sangat* after 6 June 1984. But how is it that prior to this date nobody ever mentioned it? One heard the names of Sant Longowal and Bhindranwale as someone superior to him.

The discredited appointees now want to impose their newly-found will on the Sikh *sangat.* This is really the time for the Sikh intellectual to 'break out of his mental block and come out of his home as well and lead the community – to instil in it some common sense.

The Akalis were not really concerned with the welfare of the Sikhs; they could not see beyond their own political concerns. In the early 80s many of the Sikhs who lived outside Punjab used to tell me that the movement for Khalistan had made them feel insecure. Some of them were bureaucrats and each time they went to Punjab, they were asked if they were indeed going back to Khalistan. Or they were continually mocked about when Khalistan would be born.

I went to see Tohra about this fear. I told him that I had come to see him as a Sikh and not as a politician. But when I expressed concern about what Sikhs outside Punjab felt, he merely said that nothing could be achieved without *qurbani.*

This was not too different from what Bhindranwale voiced in his tapes. The Sikhs who lived outside Punjab were traitors for him. 'Let them die,' he had said, 'for they do not do our work.'

Tohra does not believe in any religion. He has ruined the image of the Sikhs. In fact, I hold him responsible for the tarnished image of the Sikhs. I cannot stay in the Harmandir Sahib or in the SGPC without his permission.

Why should there be an office of a political party in any gurdwara? Nine crore of SGPC money was misused for political purposes.

I would also hold the leadership of the Akali Dal responsible for what has happened because they turned out to be so weak. They had known Tohra's game all along and did nothing letting themselves be outmanoeuvred by the extremists. Towards the end they even appealed to the government to save them because they feared that the extremists would blow up the gurdwara.

Tohra is really the evil genius behind a lot of the disruption which has taken place in Punjab, in fact both Tohra and Harkishan Singh Surjeet. The latter has been chief adviser to Tohra since at least 1978. The way he brought Harkishan Singh Surjeet into the Rajya Sabha appears most illogical. Why should the Akalis support a CPM leader as a Rajya Sabha member rather than one of their own men?

When Harkishan Singh Surjeet began to criticize the Akalis and project the CPM, Badal realized Tohra's game. His eyes were opened. Tohra was responsible for planting CPM card holders as *Pracharaks*, (junior *granthis*) in nearly 75 per cent of the gurdwaras in Haryana and Punjab during the late-70s.

The education department, as such, was dominated by the CPM since the mid-70s. But the CPM had not been too successful in spreading their culture through education in Punjab because those very school children who had been brainwashed by the CPM teachers in school would return home each day (usually to land-owning families) and all that brainwashing would be nullified.

Thus, the strategy of 'if you cannot lick them join them' began to be implemented. Sikh religion also teaches that everybody is equal: there is no high or low, everybody should help each other. This outlook on life married well with the CPM message. In 20 years these juniors would become head *granthis.* Politics would then really be played from the pulpit. The CPM would ride piggy-back on the provincial parties.

The reason why I keep coming back to the point of the Akalis not being sincere about doing something for Punjab is the fact that during their three years in power from 1977 onwards, they were silent about the demands which suddenly emerged after they lost the elections in 1980. Never had there been such an opportunity for the Akalis. They were in power in Punjab and at the centre. In the Janata ministry, there were three Akali ministers: Prakash Singh Badal (until he went to Punjab as chief minister), Surjit Singh Barnala, and Dhana Singh Gulshan. In fact, when Mr Barnala was in charge of agriculture and irrigation at the centre, why did they not think of solving these problems? Why did they not do something about Thein Dam? Would the SYL (Sultlej-Yamuna Link) solve the issue? It would still not have been enough. Why did they not ask for an atomic power station?

The welfare of Punjab was certainly not the main concern of the Akalis. When the 400th anniversary of Amritsar was celebrated in 1978 why did the Akalis not declare it a 'holy city'? Why did they think of all these things once they were out of power?

They are always ready to criticize Mrs Gandhi. Morarji Desai never even talked to them. At least Mrs Gandhi listens to them.

What will happen in the future is difficult to say. Many of the Akalis are in jail. There is yawning gap in the leadership. One can only pray that a sensible leadership emerges and that it will pass from the *sants* to educated and far-sighted people.

Efforts should now be made to do something about the youth who were misguided because of increasing unemployment. Bhindranwale was able to influence the AISSF boys by convincing them that once Hindus were sent out of Punjab there would be enough jobs for them. False hopes were aroused in the youth, a false vision was given to them.

In the rural areas, farmers have suffered and agriculture should now be given maximum help. Youth should be employed in agro-based industries. It is absolutely essential to set up small industries in rural areas. Rural credit should be increased. The farmer has really been given low priority until now. To help bridge the increasing chasm between Hindus and Sikhs all secular forces should come forward.

The Akalis hate me. They think that I am anti-Sikh. I am not anti-Sikh: I am anti-Akali. They have ruined the image of the Sikhs. For the first time the differences between the Hindus and Sikhs has taken such an ugly turn.

We did have the Fateh Singh agitation; but hatred was never there. The Sikhs are known for their tolerance. They respect other religions. Guru Nanak Dev even sent people to Mecca. The Sikhs are very liberal; but, these Akalis made us feel as if we were intolerant.

The Akali agitation has done incalculable damage to the Sikh community. The Akalis now call me a traitor to the Sikh community. There is so much pressure on me from my friends as well. But I am confident that I am right and I hope that other Sikhs will see reason and try to face facts.

Where is the danger to the Sikh community? What was the need for the *dharamyudh*? Who is asking us to change? Who is converting us?

The extremists converted us into a community of cowards. Bhindranwale was more worried about the Sikhs who were not with him; he felt that the Hindus were much easier to handle. Consequently 55 of every 100 people killed were Sikhs. Sikhs were killed to silence us.

We are now shouting and screaming after the army action. We say our sentiments are hurt. These are hollow sentiments. Where were these sentiments when Hindus and Sikhs were being killed? Why were we silent when Hindus were pulled out from buses and shot like dogs on the street?

Actually the blow to the Sikh community has been quite profound. We are a very proud community. We thought we were the cat's whiskers, the saviour of all. But now it was seen that we did not have the guts to face the situation. We, the Sikhs, should have been the ones to throw Bhindranwale out of the premises of the Golden Temple. We are now finding it difficult to admit our own failure. Our so-called dynamism and bravery has disappeared.

Still, I am optimistic. Time is a great healer. The Sikhs have to search within themselves. The healing touch should come from the Sikhs themselves. I must search myself for a healing touch, and finding it, must help others to do so.

Terrorists in the Temple

TAVLEEN SINGH

It was a week after Operation Bluestar and the Golden Temple still smelled faintly of death. The bodies that had been laid out in rows in white marble corridors had been removed but the temple had the atmosphere of a mortuary. Everything was cold, white, empty. Even the soldiers, who wandered around barefoot, heads covered with handkerchiefs, went about their work with a chilling silence as if talking was somehow forbidden.

We had come to Amritsar by road and in the villages and towns we passed through the Bhindranwale myth had assumed alarming proportions. His 'martyrdom' had made him a saint to many and superhuman to many others. There were those who believed that he had not died and that he had escaped to Pakistan dressed as a soldier. Those who believed that he had died spoke of his *shaheedi* in hushed tones and said it had taken over 70 bullets to kill him. Outside, in the Punjab countryside, his presence had loomed over everything more ominously than ever before, but inside the temple it was his absence that was everywhere as if an era had ended. A chapter of history closed.

In the days when he was alive it was not possible to enter the Golden Temple without becoming instantly aware of the existence of Bhindranwale. He had stamped everything with his own slightly warped brand of Sikhism and because he always thought of himself as an undeclared heir to Guru Gobind Singh. He created inside the temple the medieval world that must have existed in the days of the tenth guru.

The youths in his entourage dressed almost invariably in traditional loose kurtas, caught at the waist by a sash, and the long shorts associated with the Khalsa uniform. Their turbans tended to be blue, black or saffron and along with their Stenguns and carbines most of them carried traditional weapons like *kirpans*, swords or spears.

It was like entering a portion of medieval India caught in a time warp and a little as if Khalistan had already come into being and this was its capital.

It was the day after DIG, Avtar Singh Atwal, was shot dead outside the Golden Temple on 25 April 1983 that I met Jarnail Singh Bhindranwale for the first time. He lived at the time in room 47 of the Guru Nanak Niwas and the entire building had been taken over by his entourage. Armed youths had been positioned at strategic points but these were early days and the atmosphere of violence, that later hung over the gurdwara like a pall, was not yet perceptible.

Bhindranwale was busy so I was ushered into a sort of anteroom, adjoining his in which a couple of young, rather pretty women, wearing *kirpans* and their hair knotted on top of their heads under their *duppattas* attended to various domestic chores. One stirred boiling hot milk in a stainless steel cauldron of enormous proportions and another was involved in bathing a small boy. The room had the congenial atmosphere of a village home. Hot milk was served to everyone with a herb called *banuksha* in it. Bhindranwale was rabidly against intoxicants so even tea was forbidden.

After about fifteen minutes Rachhpal Singh, Bhindranwale's bespectacled, scholarly-looking secretary, arrived and indicated that I should follow him into the next room. Bhindranwale reclining on a bed appeared to be giving a discourse on religion to a rather large group of elderly Sikh men. After a cursory greeting he ignored me and continued with his lecture. The room had two or three beds in it, a large picture of Guru Gobind Singh and a couple of tape recorders.

Finally he turned to me and said that I could now ask him what I wanted to. What did he have to say about the murder of DIG Atwal? 'The Sikh does not believe in violence especially not in front of the Harmandir Sahib; no Sikh can ever believe in this. This has been done deliberately to make the *dharamyudh morcha* unsuccessful. It is a conspiracy to lay the grounds for the police to enter the Darbar Sahib. This could only be the work of the government.'

Did he not think Punjab was well set on a road to destruction? 'It is up to the government to decide what it wants to do, it is in their hands to bring peace or destruction. It is the government's job not mine. I am for peace; I believe there should be peace in the country.'

There were a few more terse answers to questions about the *morcha*, the Anandpur Sahib Resolution and the Akalis. He liked to answer questions as briefly as possible till he was brought on to his favourite subject, the oppression of the Sikhs. It was not difficult to get him onto the subject anyway since he seemed to wait for any question that would give him a chance to get started on it.

This time it was because I asked him whether he really believed that the Sikhs had been treated unjustly. Within seconds the calm manner had disappeared and his tone changed from a disinterested drawl to something resembling the rattle of machine-gun fire. 'Do you need proof of this?' he shouted,

'Write, I'll tell you. A Sikh girl was stripped naked and paraded around Dao village by policemen. They caught a Sikh *granthi*, and a policeman sat on him and smoked bidis and spat in his mouth and put tobacco in it. The name of the Sikh was Jasbir Singh, village Chupkiti, tehsil Moga. They caught another Sikh and when they did not find anything on him, they cut his thigh, tore the flesh out and poured salt into the cut. Name: Jagir Singh, village: Ittanwali, he lives in Moga. Is this not wrong? During the Asian Games they drew a line and said that anyone with Singh attached to his name couldn't go to Delhi at all. Did they stop anyone else? Is this not injust 8ice to the Sikhs? Has anyone ever said that a *jenoi* cannot be more than a particular length. Then why is there a restriction on our religious symbol? Is this not discrimination?'

Once he got started there was no stopping him. Within seconds he had managed to whip up a frenzy. 'Call Leher Singh,' he shouted, 'You want to know what they do to the Sikhs, let me show you.' A few minutes later, a rather large man of about 30 was brought in. He was dressed in traditional Sikh clothes but his beard had been hacked off, as if with a knife. He said that he was from Jatwali village in Fazilka and that Thanedar Bicchu Ram of Sadar Police Station had held him down and chopped his beard off and told him to go and tell Bhindranwale. Six months later Bicchu Ram was shot dead by terrorists and it was then that I realized that I had witnessed the signing of the death warrant.

After several visits to the Golden Temple it slowly became clear that this was how the hit list was prepared. Bhindranwale dispensed his own version of justice. People would come from all over Punjab with complaints against policemen, officials, judges or just other people. Their complaints would be carefully noted down by Racchpal Singh and action taken of one kind or another. If the complaints were against Hindus the punishment was generally death; Sikhs could sometimes be let off if they came and begged forgiveness. If someone received a favour from Bhindranwale then it was understood that in future he would consider himself one of his men to be called on if the need arose. By the end he managed to establish a network of spies in the villages through whom he silenced those who did not believe in him.

By the time I first met Bhindranwale he had been living inside the Golden Temple for almost a year. He moved in on 19 July 1982 after his two lieutenants Amreek Singh and Thara Singh were arrested. He seemed to have learned very quickly the art of getting headlines and by 1983 he had become a big media star. He had come a long way from those early days in 1978 when he was first discovered by an important Congress(I) member and his school friends.

Bhindranwale was born in Rode Village near Moga in 1947. His father Jathedar Joginder Singh married twice and he was the second son of the second wife. According to his family he was interested in religion from a very early age and dropped out of school after class five to concentrate on learning the Sikh scriptures. He then joined a religious group called Chakravarti Gurmat Prachar Jatha Bhindran and eventually ended up as a follower of Sant Kartar Singh of the Damdami Taxal.

This Taxal, whose headquarters are in Mehta, was founded by Baba Deep Singh, a legendary Sikh hero after whom the Baba Deep Singh Gurdwara in Amritsar is named. It has been built at the spot where he according to legend, was beheaded while fighting Ahmed Shah Abdali. He is said to have held his head in his hand and fought on till the Golden Temple, nearly a kilometre away, and finally fell in the Parikrama. It was he who founded the Damdami Taxal as a school for teaching Sikh scriptures and over the years it came to be recognized as an institution which taught the essence of Sikhism.

Bhindranwale took over from Sant Kartar Singh, Amreek Singh's father. Amreek Singh should have been the natural heir since he was brought up in the Taxal and groomed as its next head but he was at the time of his father's death studying

Punjabi literature at Khalsa College, Amritsar, and already deeply involved in the politics of the All India Sikh Students Federation and he encouraged Bhindranwale to become the next head of the Taxal. In those early days Bhindranwale was strongly influenced by Amreek Singh who, it is believed, had hoped to manipulate him for his political ends.

Bhindranwale took over as head of the Damdami Taxal in 1977 and almost immediately started having problems with the Nirankaris. Contrary to the popular belief that he took the offensive, senior police sources in Punjab admit that the provocation came in fact from a Nirankari official who started harassing Bhindranwale and his men.

There were two or three Nirankaris in key positions in Punjab in those days and they were powerful enough to be able to create quite a lot of trouble. The Nirankaris also received patronage from Delhi which made Sikh organizations like Bhindranwale's and the Akhand Kirtani Jatha, headed then by Bibi Amarjit Kaur's husband, Fauja Singh, hate them even more.

The enmity culminated in the Sikh-Nirankari clash outside the Golden Temple on 13 April 1978 (Baisakhi) in which 13 Sikhs, including Fauja Singh, were killed. The following day the Babbar Khalsa was formed as a breakaway faction of the Akhand Kirtani Jatha, created with the specific aim of taking revenge on the Nirankaris. It was also from this point that the Akhand Kirtani Jatha and Bhindranwale parted company because Bibi Amarjit Kaur felt that Bhindranwale had shown cowardice by not turning up for the anti-Nirankari demonstration despite having vowed to lead it.

It was shortly after the Baisakhi incident that Bhindranwale started being noticed in Delhi. Mrs Gandhi had now been out of power for a year and, thanks to the Janata government, she was now seriously thinking in terms of a comeback. When casting his eyes in the direction of Punjab, the Congress(I) member is believed to have confided to some of his friends that since the Akali Dal was doing quite well the only way to break their hold would be to try and find some religious leader who they could build up as the real representative of Sikh interests.

The amateur politicians then started their search for a *sant*. They approached at least twenty who refused their offers of money and fame and finally turned to Bhindranwale who in those days was becoming quite well known in the village around Mehta for his zeal in converting people back to the true faith. He and a group of his youthful supporters would tramp through the dust of village streets, armed with sticks and full of aggression against anyone who looked as if he may have clipped a few discreet inches off an unruly beard or may have imbibed an intoxicant of any kind. His philosophy in six words was *Nashey chaddo. Amrit chhako. Gursikh bano.* (Give up addictions. Take Amrit. Become good Sikhs.)

One of these new political recruits remembers that it was quite difficult to persuade Bhindranwale to see that there was more to life than his simple, rustic philosophy. He remembers that Bhindranwale had said that it would be very wrong to divide up the Sikhs which is what their strategy would do and he also remembers him saying often, *Kaka sarkar naal ladna bahut aukha haunda hai* (Son, it is a very difficult thing to take on the government).

The Congress(I) leader and his friends were, however, masters at making offers that were impossible to refuse and Sant Jarnail Singh and his men, heavily financed by the Congress(I), fought the Shiromani Gurdwara Prabandhak Committee (SGPC) elections against the Akali Dal in 1979. This was the birth of the Dal Khalsa. The Akali Dal won all but 4 of the 150 seats and among the other groups who fought against them were Dr Jagjit Singh Chauhan and the Khalistan lobby and Amreek Singh as a member of the AISSF.

After the humiliating defeat of all his candidates Bhindranwale turned to his Congress(I) mentors and said that this was clearly a sign from the gods that what he was doing was not right and so he decided to go back to preaching Sikhism instead. Once more the persuaders got to work and Bhindranwale did what he could to assist the Congress(I) in the 1980 elections.

Then on 24 April 1980 Baba Gurbachan Singh was murdered and Bhindranwale made no efforts to hide his approval. He was taken in for interrogation but could not be implicated. The following year on 9 August 1981 came the murder of Lala Jagat Narain and Bhindranwale's nephew was one of the suspected killers. He himself was believed to have been involved and there was the extraordinary drama of his arrest. The authorities allowed him to decide where and how this would take place and he took the opportunity to demonstrate his first show of strength – 100,000 people gathered at gurdwara Gurdarshan Prakash, his Mehta headquarters, and at least 20 were killed in the violence that followed his arrest. After which he was released unconditionally.

By then he appears to have understood that the name of the game was being in the right place at the right time and that Amritsar being the political centre was a better choice than Mehta and so it was from Amritsar that he started his anti-tobacco movement and the agitation for getting 'holy city' status for the old part of Amritsar. Then came the final move following Amreek Singh's arrest after which the Akali Dal appears to have also understood the importance of Amritsar for they picked up their dying *morcha* and shifted it from Kapoori to join hands with Bhindranwale in a new *dharamyudh morcha.*

In retrospect when one looks at the events that led to Operation Bluestar it is clear that the first flashpoint was the killing of DIG Atwal. Several policemen were prepared to swear that they had seen a youth wearing a greyish kurta and a black turban run inside the Golden Temple after shooting the officer dead at point blank range. Later there were even those who said that the DIG was followed while he was still in the Parikrama and that his murder was without doubt the result of a plot hatched inside the Golden Temple. The police was of the view that they should have been allowed to enter and arrest the suspect.

All the factions that inhabited the gurdwara at that point were, on the other hand, convinced that the murder was a government plot devised to find an excuse to enter the temple complex. Nevertheless, although the possibility of a police entry inside the gurdwara did start being discussed, nobody lost much sleep over it and life carried on in a fairly carefree fashion.

The extremists and the moderates seemed to spend long, idle days doing nothing. Bhindranwale never gave any audience till around 10 a.m. and generally began the day with a trip to the Harmandir Sahib accompanied by his Stengun toting bodyguards. Afterwards he would meet the journalists (nobody was ever refused an interview) and other outsiders who had come to see him. He loved the sound of his own discourses and could talk endlessly on being a good Sikh, or being a good Hindu or on religion in general.

While on the subject of politics he would never miss an opportunity to make a snide remark about Longowal but apart from this there was no overt tension although the Akalis spent most of their time debating whether Bhindranwale was still being paid by the Congress(I) or not.

In the afternoons everyone rested and a silence would descend over the place as the gurdwara was turned over for a few brief hours to the pilgrims who would come and sit on the white hot marble and gaze at the Harmandir Sahib or sit in shaded spots and listen to the soft notes of *kirtan*.

Then suddenly at around 4 p.m. the whole place would burst into life. Political slogans, shouted over loudspeakers, would drown out the *kirtan* and hundreds of volunteers wearing saffron bands on their heads would march from the Manji Sahib to the Akal Takht where they took vows to give their lives for the *dharamyudh morcha*.

A priest would make the volunteers swear that if the dictator of the *morcha* sent for them at any time they would come whether it meant leaving their own wedding ceremony or even the last rites of a loved one.

The *jathas* leaving to court arrest was the event of the day and the volunteers were often addressed by Longowal, Bhindranwale and other important leaders. Shouting the Sikh battle cry they would leave the gurdwara through what was called the 'Street of the Serais', where the Akali Dal office and Guru Nanak Niwas are.

Once the *jatha* left peace would descend on the Golden Temple again and dusk would see the place converted once more into just a place of worship.

In those early days Bhindranwale and Harmandir Singh Sandhu were the two most sought-after people in the extremist camp till the rediscovery of Khalistan secretary-general, Balbir Singh Sandhu. For a few weeks in the middle of 1983 he took the centre stage when the press suddenly remembered that the so-called Khalistan headquarters were in the Guru Nanak Niwas and this reminded the government and the opposition about something they should have known anyway which is that Balbir Singh Sandhu had been living in room 32 since 1980. It was from here, in a much publicized event, that he issued the first blue and gold Khalistan passport on 13 April 1981 to Gopal Singh Shahid, a farmer from Mehta.

The Guru Nanak Niwas, during the days that it was inhabited by Bhindranwale and his men, was like a rabbit warren of dingy, dismal rooms in which you expected every moment to come across some armed criminal or some illegal activity. The arsenals were believed to be in the string of heavily padlocked rooms on the ground floor but these were out of bounds to outsiders.

Room 32, the Khalistan headquarters-cum-residence of the secretary-general, was at the end of a damp corridor full of bathrooms. The only nice thing about the room was that it had a view, through a barred window, of the Manji Sahib Gurdwara with the Golden Temple in the background.

Balbir Singh Sandhu hardly ever left the room. His food used to be brought up to him and he had a small electric stove, placed on one of the window-sills, on which he heated tea for guests.

The Khalistan secretary-general was a large, affable man in his mid-fifties. He spoke very chaste Punjabi and had a world-view based on a strange mixture of progressive ideas borrowed from Marx and some very rigid beliefs based on Sikhism. Before he became actively involved in the Khalistan struggle he was a writer of progressive plays and books. In 1970 he published a play called 'Lahu Dhara' which received considerable acclaim.

The refreshing thing about Sandhu was that, whereas Longowal clothed his statements in ambiguity and Bhindranwale talked in parables, he always said exactly what he meant. He believed that even the so-called moderates in the Golden Temple were in the final analysis fighting for Khalistan and would have to say so sooner or later. Although Bhindranwale had been hesitant to admit a link with the Khalistan secretary-general, Sandhu said openly that they met each other almost every evening.

He believed that Bhindranwale had helped the Khalistan movement greatly by encouraging Sikh fundamentalism and the Akalis had made a major contribution with the resurrection of the Anandpur Sahib Resolution.

He said, 'Sant Jarnail Singhji Khalsa Bhindranwale has drawn the Sikh masses back towards the gurbani and given them the strength to go back to following their old traditions, this has helped to create in their hearts a desire for Khalistan. Where the Akali Dal is concerned, we feel that this *morcha* in the name of the Anandpur Sahib Resolution has strengthened the determination among the people to have Khalsa Raj. If the Akalis betray the *morcha*, then the people will lose faith in them and there will be a direct wave in favour of Khalistan.'

Sandhu was convinced that nothing would stand in the way of Khalistan becoming a reality. If the army entered the Golden Temple, he believed, that the process of formation of Khalistan would only be helped along the way.

It is difficult to pinpoint exactly when the tension between the moderate and the extremist camps began to come out into the open but by September 1983 the facade of peaceful coexistence had begun to crumble,

The Akali Dal, attended in July that year, an opposition parties meeting on Punjab, arranged by Democratic Socialist Party president, Mr H.N. Bahuguna, in Delhi and agreed to a plan under which the water dispute would go to the Supreme Court and Chandigarh to Punjab.

Inside the Golden Temple, however, a campaign was mounted against them by the extremists who mocked them for even thinking of a solution that did not include all the demands in the Anandpur Sahib Resolution. In what looked like an almost deliberate attempt to destroy any alliance they might be considering with the national opposition parties Bhindranwale made his first blatantly anti-Hindu statement around September when he said he would kill 5,000 Hindus if the police did not release a minibus of his that had been impounded.

Bhindranwale was clearly making a conscious effort to embarrass the moderates into either taking a hardline or accepting a back seat in the agitation. A whisper campaign started in the Golden Temple against 'the weakness and treachery' of Longowal.

It was around this time that dead bodies started appearing in the sewer in a street directly behind the Guru Nanak Niwas. The first one was discovered some time in August or September when a terrible stench hung over the street and filtered through to the SGPC office. Bhan Singh, the SGPC general-secretary, telephoned the senior superintendent of police and reqested a police party to come and 'look in the sewer where there appeared to be a body.'

The police party, after taking special permission from the SGPC to enter 'their territory,' opened up the manhole and fished out the body of a youth who appeared to have been tortured to death.

In the next few weeks three or four more bodies were fished out of the same sewer in similar conditions. Inquiries inside the Golden Temple were answered with sullen stares in the direction of the Guru Nanak Niwas. Those who were prepared to talk only did so in whispers. They said that the victims had betrayed Bhindranwale and had been tied in sacks and beaten to death. Nobody dared to even remember their names. They were just traitors.

The police, of course, could do nothing at all because the murders had taken place in 'their (extremists') territory.' A section of the Brahma Boota Bazaar had already become part of extremist territory, as had a couple of streets in the immediate vicinity of the temple. The police behaved as if they needed a passport to enter this area. One senior officer said he had tried driving into the Brahma Boota Bazaar late one night but the minute he got within firing range of the Golden Temple's entrance he had noticed a machine-gun pointed at him from the roof of the Akal Rest House.

Slowly Bhindranwale's ideology of violence began to become the official policy of the Golden Temple. Longowal seemed to retire deeper into his lair and was hardly ever seen in public. If the SGPC and the Akalis disapproved of what was happening they kept it to themselves. The only person who seemed to have one leg in either camp was Gurcharan Singh Tohra, the SGPC president. He was clearly at home in both the camps.

By September 1983 Amreek Singh and Thara Singh had been inadvertently released. They were acquitted of some of the charges against them and were meant to have been rearrested, on other charges, the minute they left court but, for some mysterious reason, the police officer who was to have made the arrests did not show up and they were given enough time to be whisked off to the Golden Temple in a brand new Fiat car that had been waiting outside the court.

A year in jail had convinced Amreek Singh that the moderates in the Akali party were wrong and that Bhindranwale was right. Despite this, however, to the very end he retained a gentle, rather polite manner and never exhibited the venom and fanaticism of Bhindranwale or Harmandir Singh Sandhu.

Having been brought up in the religious atmosphere of the Damdami Taxal he had, even as a student, the mannerisms of a Sikh priest. Those who were students with him at Khalsa College remember that he wore traditional clothes even then. Ironically, his advent into Akali politics was in the moderate camp and he was close to Prakash Singh Badal.

After he became president of the AISSF it is believed to have been Tohra who became his mentor and urged him to sever the student body's links with the moderates. Right up to the time of his arrest in 1982, Amreek Singh was considered a moderating influence on Bhindranwale.

From the moment he came out of jail, however, it became clear that if there was a choice between the extremists and the moderates, the AISSF would stick with Bhindranwale.

On 20 September 1983 the students' body, officially meant to be a branch of the Akali Dal, held a meeting in the Manji Sahib Gurdwara which turned into a massive show of support for Sant Jarnail Singh.

From the dawn of that day an endless stream of trucks started pouring into the complex and parking outside the *serais.* Truck after truck unloaded hundreds of armed youths shouting '*jo boley so nihal, sat sri akal.*' Some carried guns, others carried hockey sticks or lathis. Nobody came unarmed.

Then the leaders started arriving, each of them accompanied by armed bodyguards so that the dais became a virtual forest of Stenguns and rifles.

Longowal made one of his rare public appearances and the meeting was also attended by senior Akali leaders, senior SGPC officials, former army men like Major General J.S. Bhullar, journalists like the *Akali Patrika* editor, Bharpoor Singh Balbir and most district presidents of the AISSF. The star of the show was Bhindranwale in spotless white and carrying a huge sword in a scabbard of gold thread.

For some inexplicable reason the meeting went virtually unnoticed in the national press and by the government although at least 80 per cent of the speakers spoke as openly for Khalistan as it was possible to do without giving it a name. Even Longowal said, '*We say raj karega Khalsa.* Well it is to rule that we are fighting and it will be a Raj of the kind that Guru Nanak dreamed about.' He added that this was the fourth struggle that the Sikhs had taken part in – the first against the Mughals, the second against the British, the third against the Emergency and now the fourth for 'our own freedom.'

Bhindranwale's sense of morality was so warped that between speeches, the audience was made to listen to anti-government and anti-Hindu songs in which concepts like non-violence were mocked and sneering remarks made about Gandhi. 'Our Bapu (Guru Gobind Singh) had arms and fine arrows and their Bapu had an old man's walking stick.' Jathedar Jagdev Singh Talwandi, who was by now closer to Bhindranwale than Longowal, and the editor of the *Akali Patrika*, Bharpoor Singh Balbir were arrested that day for making secessionist speeches but no attention was paid to the speeches by moderates like Longowal and Bibi Rajinder Kaur, the former MP, who said, 'The slavery that we faced under the British has been nothing compared to the slavery we have faced since 1947.'

The message of the meeting was that the extremists were now in control and Balbir Singh Sandhu who heard the proceedings from his room overlooking the Manji Sahib Gurdwara commented afterwards, 'Sooner or later every Akali leader will be forced to ask for Khalistan because this is what the people want.'

Once the daily *jatha* had left for the Kotwali police station, this time with more than normal ardour, the stars of the show repaired to various dimly-lit rooms in the Guru Nanak Niwas. In one such room, amid streams of drying turbans, I met Amreek Singh for the first time. He was relaxing with Harmandir Singh Sandhu and several other AISSF members and conversation inevitably turned to 'threats' to the very existence of Sikhism.

Amreek Singh said the Sikh children were losing ties with their roots because they went to schools where from day one were taught about Hinduism and Hindu culture. 'They are told that Gandhi is their Bapu and Nehru their Chacha. Their Bapu is Guru Gobind Singh not Gandhi.'

Sandhu produced a textbook for class eighth children in Delhi schools and turned to a page which said that Guru Gobind Singh had started fighting the Mughals because they killed his father. 'This is the kind of rubbish our children are being taught and they tell us they are not threatening our culture,' he said. This was the first of many similar discussions with Sandhu and Amreek Singh most of which ended up with them saying that although they were not fighting for Khalistan, it would become inevitable unless the Sikhs could have a portion of India (as envisaged in the Anandpur Sahib Resolution) in which their culture would be dominant over Hindu culture.

The story of Harmandir Singh Sandhu is a strange one. He was one of the two or three people very close to Bhindranwale. He was the most outspoken of the lot, an articulate champion of Sikh militancy and yet in the early years of his political life he is believed to have been very close to Raghunandan Lal Bhatia, the president of Punjab Congress(I), and is even said to have campaigned for police commissioner P.S. Bhinder's wife during the 1980 elections.

He was the son of a small, quite well-to-do farmer Rattan Singh Mattia and became general-secretary of the AISSF at the same time that Amreek Singh became its president. He studied law at Khalsa College.

Before hiding in the Golden Temple, he had spent a year in jail and had 20 police cases against him. Sandhu was articulate and the only member of the inner circle who spoke fluent English, so his main job in the temple was to act as an interpreter for Bhindranwale. In one of the conversations we had he explained the rise of the military *sant* by saying, 'You see, for a while Sikh youths had turned their face away from Sikhism, mainly because the Akali leadership had become passive – they had adjusted to the so-called democratic system. To be a Sikh and to be young necessarily means to be adventurous. Sant Bhindranwale offered us the adventure.'

Slowly the venom that was being spewed out every day from the Golden Temple started to get into the very blood of Punjab and this culminated inevitably and horribly in the killings of six Hindu bus passengers in Dhilwan village, near Jullundur on 5 October 1983. The men were singled out by Sikh terrorists and shot dead for the simple reason that they were Hindu.

The following day a terrified administration handed in its resignation and the state was put under president's rule. While the whole country reacted with shock and horror, the extremists in the Golden Temple showed neither remorse nor sorrow.

Naturally, they denied that the killers were hiding in the gurdwara, as the police claimed, but when asked what he felt about what had happened Bhindranwale replied ominously, 'Six Hindus are killed and the government falls. Two hundred Sikhs have been gunned down by the police and nothing has been done. This shows that to the government, Hindu lives are more important than Sikh lives.'

Bhindranwale, despite being the prophet of hate that he was, had managed to touch some kind of raw nerve in that nebulous, barely comprehended phenomenon called the Sikh identity crisis and his sympathizers were not all terrorists. Around the time that president's rule was declared I met a former civil servant Gurtej Singh who was very close to the Sant and believed, in fact, to be one of his chief ideologues. Gurtej Singh was in the Indian Administrative Service's Andhra cadre for ten years and resigned in November 1982 after propagating the theory that the Sikhs were a separate nation.

Gurtej Singh was the exact antithesis of his comrades in the Golden Temple. He had grown up in the privileged world of upper-middle class India, a world of public schools, expensive colleges and financial security. He lived in Chandigarh in a large, well-furnished house whose only concession to the cause was an enormous picture of the Sikh hero Banda Bahadur which hung in the drawing room.

Gurtej, more than anyone else in the Bhindranwale camp, represented the conflicts of the Sikh identity crisis. His only explanation for having sacrificed a career in the Indian Administrative Service was that he believed fundamentally that the Sikhs were a separate people to the Hindus and that they could never get a fair deal in the existing political setup. 'If Ireland were to be made a part of Russia and then it were said that in Ireland there is one man one vote, it can elect a government and therefore it should submit to the government of the majority, would it be fair? You see we are facing the tyranny of the majority. Like-minded people can get together and elect their own universally acceptable government. But not when they are poles apart.'

He would quote Guru Nanak to prove that Sikhs were not Hindus. It was the first guru who said *'Na hum Hindu, na Mussalman,'* he would point out, and add that to say Sikhs were Hindus was like calling all Christians Jews because *Christ had been Jewish.*

Bhindranwale, to him, was almost a messiah and could do no wrong. He even absolved him of the terrorism charge, saying, 'All I can say is why does the government not manage to catch a single person in these incidents? Even those men of his whom they caught, have been released. If Bhindranwale is capable of organizing terrorism on such a scale and the government can do nothing about it, they should hand over power to him.'

By the end of 1983, the scale of terrorism had become truly astounding and it was beginning to look as if Bhindranwale really was the ruler of Punjab, but inside the Golden Temple his opponents had decided to take a stand. Longowal, who for months had watched silently, as Bhindranwale became the de facto leader of the *dharamyudh morcha* suddenly seemed to feel the need to fight back.

As if realizing finally that you cannot fight Stenguns with words he turned to the Babbar Khalsa and Bibi Amarjit Kaur for armed assistance and on 15 December a civil war broke out between the extremists and the moderates which lasted till the very end.

Early on the morning of 15 December, six armed youths belonging to the Babbar Khalsa group entered the Guru Nanak Niwas which was recognized as Bhindranwale territory. The Babbars lived mainly in the Guru Ram Das Serai and the Akal Rest House, situated on the other side of the Teja Singh Samundari Hall. According to Balbir Singh Sandhu who witnessed what happened, from room 32, 'These youths came in looking for a fight. They marched into some rooms occupied by Sant Jarnail Singh's men and told them to get out. They said the rooms were theirs.'

Bhindranwale had at least 200 armed men staying in the Guru Nanak Niwas at the time but instead of fighting the Babbars, he and his followers packed their belongings and moved by that afternoon into the Akal Takht.

Bhindranwale said later, 'I did not want to desecrate the sanctity of the Harmandir Sahib by allowing a fight to take place, that is why I moved.'

In the moderate camp, however, they said that the move was a political stunt and the Babbar Khalsa, who were now ironically part of the moderate camp, saw it as a yet another indication of Bhindranwale's cowardice. 'Six unarmed Babbars managed to scare away 200 armed men,' scoffed Jathedar Sukhdev Singh who headed the Babbar Khalsa.

About two days later people in the Ram Das Serai heard shots being fired in one of the rooms and rushed in to find Santokh Singh, a follower of Bhindranwale, dying in a pool of blood. The extremist camp swore that they saw a member of the Akali Dal youth wing coming out of the room. Within hours the victim's relations had collected outside the SGPC office and started shouting that the Akalis were responsible for what had happened. The dead man's mother beat her breast and said Longowal had done nothing to help her whereas Bhindranwale had immediately promised financial assistance.

Inside the Teja Samundari Hall, which housed the Akali Dal and SGPC offices, there was little sympathy forthcoming. In fact, when a senior SGPC official was told about the rumour that it was a member of the Akali Dal who had been accused of committing the murder he said angrily, 'What about the men they have killed? What about them?'

Once again it was left to Tohra to act as mediator. He flitted between the roof of the Guru Ram Das Building, where Bhindranwale had now taken to holding court in the December sunshine, and the Teja Singh Samundari Hall opposite. There were confabulations and secret meetings and ostensible efforts to resolve the dispute but the battle lines remained drawn with the Akalis, the Akhand Kirtani Jatha, the Babbar Khalsa and the SGPC on one side and Bhindranwale, the AISSF and the youths from his Taxal on the other.

As a result of the bloodless coup in the Guru Nanak Niwas the Babbar Khalsa suddenly emerged from the shadows. Jathedar Sukhdev Singh, a youth of about 28, who dressed like a Nihang, started requesting journalists to come up and meet him in a small, sunless room in the Akal Rest House. He would talk about how it was really the Babbars who had killed most of the Nirankaris so far and how they would continue to kill them (the toll was already around 40) because they followed the dictate of the Akal Takht and they were only abiding by an edict *(hukumnamas)* issued by them.

The extraordinary thing about the Babbars, (there were about 40 of them) was that they could come and go from the Golden Temple as they pleased because the polce had no idea who they were. They never had themselves photographed.

Sukhdev Singh said that his organization had nothing to do with the Akali Dal or Bibi Amarjit Kaur but it was six Babbars, armed with Stenguns, who guarded her room in a portion of the Akal Takht, quite close to where Bhindranwale lived

She had agreed to meet me but I was asked to wait because some 'intellectuals' from Chandigarh were inside talking to her. I was led into a large hall in which her bodyguards also sat. It was a freezing December morning so they sat huddled on the floor under thick quilts, with only their Stenguns and rifles showing.

There was a lot of snickering going on over how Bhindranwale had 'fled' from the Guru Nank Niwas and a lot of remarks about how he was a bad Sikh because he practised untouchability, vegetarianism and other things that had nothing to do with Sikhism. They also felt that since he allowed people to touch his feet he had set himself as a guru which was completely forbidden in Sikhism.

Conversation turned to weapons and they said that Bhindranwale and his men had enough guns to arm a batallion. There were also some light-hearted complaints about how difficult it was for them (the Babbars) to obtain guns and how nice it would be if they could lay their hands on some of Dhirendra Brahmachari's Spanish guns.

Bibi Amarjit Kaur lived in a room which was constantly filled with the sound of *kirtan* from the Golden Temple of which there was a perfect view. She was a short, fat woman who retained the stern, spinsterish manner of the headmistress she had once been. She taught for several years in an Amritsar girls school but gave up to come and stay in the gurdwara where she wanted to listen to *kirtan* and find peace.

The Bibi, as she was always referred to, did not like Bhindranwale because she never seemed to have forgiven him for not having led the anti-Nirankari demonstration in which her husband was killed. She believed that the Nirankaris would not have become violent had he been there. She was not anti-Hindu in the sense that Bhindranwale was but in every other sense she was as much of a hardliner as he was. According to her, 'If the centre wants peace in Punjab then they must fulfil the demands listed in the Anandpur Sahib Resolution. Except for four subjects (defence, foreign relations, currency and general communication) the state must control everything else and the Sikhs must rule. If the centre does not agree to this then there will be Khalistan.'

The Bibi believed with a fanatical conviction in the 'mission' for which her husband started the Akhand Kirtani Jatha. The mission was to fight the threat to Sikhism posed by sects like the Nirankaris, the Neeldharis and the Radhasoamis as well as the threat from Hindu organizations like the RSS and 'anti-Sikh people like Charan Singh.'

Like the other hardliners she believed that the Sikhs had not been given a fair deal in independent India. 'The Sikhs have been turned into slaves. Look what happened during the Asian Games. Look at the fact that only in Punjab have 47,000 people had to go to jail to try and make Punjabi the official language. Look at the fact that the Sikhs never get top jobs.'

For a while after Bhindranwale moved to the Akal Takht, it looked as if Longowal had managed to get the reins of the *morcha* back into his hands. Bhindranwale had taken to sulking on the roof of the Langar building as if he had somehow been isolated from the mainstream. The moderates, on the other hand, organized a successful state-wide *bandh* on 8 February and had even agreed tentatively to begin negotiations with the government again.

Their brief, hopeful moments centre stage were abruptly ended, however, when Hindu-Sikh violence erupted in Punjab and Haryana on 14 February. The incidents in Haryana, in which Sikhs were burned and publicly humiliated and gurdwaras were desecrated, resurrected Bhindranwale and he rose mightier than ever before because for once he had been proved right.

'Kill the Hindus who have done this.' he thundered in his speches, tape recordings of which were now being distributed in the villages. After the 14 February violence he said, 'We have tried to stick to peaceful methods but after observing these recent incidents, I think the time has come for the Sikhs to unsheathe their swords.'

He made it increasingly clear that he was against Hindu-Sikh fraternity and friendship. 'They are destroying our gurdwaras, they will not stop till we make them eat steel *channas* (gram). Arm yourselves, be prepared. There are no courts to try those who murder our guru or the Granth Sahib.' 'Our guru,' said one Sikh, 'could fight, 125,000 (*sawa lakh sey ek ladaoon*). We have calculated that with a total Hindu population of 66 crores, it comes to only 35 per Sikh. Imagine only 35, not even a hundred. So don't think of yourselves as weak.'

Outside in the city of Amritsar there was curfew, as there was in at least five other Punjab cities. The state seemed to be coming to a grinding halt and slowly the security forces started closing in on the Golden Temple.

Paramilitary pickets were now visible from the Golden Temple itself and once or twice they got close enough to provoke exchanges of fire. The undercurrent of fear and impending doom that had always existed inside the gurdwara suddenly seemed to surface. Bhindranwale's bodyguards were doubled and during his daily sojourn on the roof of the Langar armed men, wearing saffron turbans and carrying light machine-guns would position themselves on all four sides. Fortifications started coming up at strategic places and an iron fencing was erected around the main entrance to the Golden Temple. The preparations for war had begun.

Slowly the atmosphere inside the Golden Temple became charged with constant tension. Gone were the idle, endless days of former times. Now everybody seemed to be involved in doing something. Meetings were constantly being held; Amreek Singh and Harmandir Sandhu were less accessible than before and less interested in debating the righteousness of their cause. Bhindranwale himself often spent days without coming out on to the Langar roof.

At the same time exchanges of fire with the paramilitary troops became more frequent and reports started filtering in about police action in Ferozepur, Moga and other places. The one thing that never seemed to weaken however was Bhindranwale's resolve to fight back if and when the attack came. 'They will never take me alive,' he repeated over and over again.

In the meantime internal tensions also increased and the two camps were openly at war. Some time in December, Ranjit Singh, the suspected killer of the Nirankari Baba, had been persuaded to leave the Golden Temple and had been taken to Delhi where he was arrested. Huge posters, appeared all over the gurdwara, blaming the Akalis for doing this. It was clear that the enmity between Bhindranwale and Longowal was now a permanent thing.

A week before Baisakhi, the extremist camp received information from one of their contacts in the Intelligence Bureau that there was a plot to kill Bhindranwale on 13 April. Major General Jaswant Singh Bhullar, one of the former generals in the militant camp, said he warned the Sant that there would be an attempt on his life.

According to Harmandir Sandhu they immediately took precautions and in the days that followed it became almost impossible for anyone to get close enough to the Sant to take a shot at him. The extremists said that on 11 April they also got information of a secret meeting held between the Akali Dal secretary Gurcharan Singh and two Bhindranwale's supporters, Surinder Singh 'Chhinda' and his girl friend Baljit Kaur. They heard that the two were offered Rs 4 lakhs to kill the Sant and were given Rs 2 lakhs in advance.

Sandhu's version is that on Baisakhi, Baljit Kaur, carrying a pistol concealed in a bag, went up to the roof of the Langar and sat opposite Bhindranwale for at least two hours but either got too scared to shoot or did not get the chance because he was so well protected by his guards. Sandhu said, 'We noticed her sitting there and we also felt that she looked very uneasy but we didn't know why.'

In any case Baljit Kaur got up and went down to the Guru Ram Das Serai where she and 'Chhinda' are believed to have met Gurcharan Singh again who is then supposed to have told them that since they had already taken half the money they should kill someone close to the Sant.

S.S. Sodhi who was the senior commander of Bhindranwale's killer squads, and who had sometimes been seen returning after 'eliminating an enemy of Sikhism' and being greeted by the rest with sweets and garlands, was the obvious choice. In the extremist camp he was considered Bhindranwale's right-hand man in terms of implementing his orders.

'Chhinda' was sent to invite him down to the Sindhi tea shop, opposite the Serai entrance to the Golden Temple, where Baljit Kaur lay in wait.

She is believed to have then held out a bandaged thumb and asked Sodhi to examine the bandage to see if it needed redoing and while both his hands were occupied 'Chhinda' reached under the table for his pistol and shot him dead at point-blank range.

After killing Sodhi, 'Chhinda' ran off into the bazaar and escaped to his village while Baljit Kaur returned to Bhindranwale shouting that Sodhi had tried to rape her. Explaining why she did this Sandhu said, 'She knew that Santji was very strict about these things and would have taken action even against Sodhi if her charge was true.'

Baljit Kaur was then 'interrogated' by Bhindranwale's men and is said to have broken down during the interrogation and confessed on tape that they had been paid by Gurcharan Singh to kill Bhindranwale. In the process she also implicated another Bhindranwale follower called Malik Singh Bhatia.

A blackboard with 'Chhinda's' name on it was immediately put up near the entrance to the Langar building and chalked on it was the statement that he would be killed in 24 hours. Bhatia in the meantime fell at Bhindranwale's feet and begged for his life. He was spared with the ominous warning that it would only be till the end of the *morcha* and he is then said to have gone downstairs and stood near the blackboard where some Nihangs were discussing the events of the day. One of them said that 'Chhinda' would be killed soon but there was another man who was also believed to have been involved. Bhatia said it was him but that he had been forgiven by the Sant.

When the Nihangs discovered who he was, one of them pulled out a sword and hacked his arms off in full view of everyone. He was then dragged off into the Guru Ram Das Serai and killed. His body joined the growing list of bodies that were being trundled out of the temple complex in a sort of tin trunk on wheels. The bodies would be handed over either to the municipal authorities or to the dead man's relatives.

'Chhinda' was tracked down and killed that night and two days later the horribly mutilated body of Baljit Kaur, her breasts had been chopped off and there were torture marks all over, was found in a sack somewhere in Amritsar.

The extremists denied having killed her. They said it was the Akalis who had done this to prevent her giving further information about the assassination plot. Gurcharan Singh, on the other hand, denied the existence of any plot and claimed that all the characters involved in the gruesome drama were former smugglers and the killings had taken place as a result of some internal quarrel. A five-member committee set up by Longowal also absolved Gurcharan Singh but it is an indication of Bhindranwale's power that Gurcharan Singh had to resign anyway. He finally demonstrated this power when as a result of the Sodhi episode a large number of members walked out of an Akali Dal meeting in the Teja Singh Samundari Hall at the end of April and pledged their loyalty to him. Longowal had lost the battle and the war. He continued to cling on to the shreds of authority that were left to him but it was clear that the so-called moderates had become irrelevant to the *dharamyudh morcha.*

In the meantime, Bhindranwale's death squads continued to spread destruction. On 28 March the Delhi Gurdwara Management Committee president, H.S. Manchanda, was killed at one of Delhi's busiest traffic intersections. Two weeks later on 16 April, 38 railway stations in Punjab were set on fire in a carefully synchronized pre-dawn operation. An organization called the Dashmesh Regiment took credit for both acts of terrorism and it became clear that a trained military mind was behind them.

Bhindranwale had no dearth of military minds to call on. In December 1982 when Sant Longowal called a convention of ex-servicemen inside the Golden Temple, 170 officers over the rank of colonel were among the approximately 5,000 ex-soldiers who came forward.

When the mysterious Dashmesh Regiment made its appearance, however, all fingers seemed to point to a frail, embittered former war hero, Major General Shabeg Singh. In military circles they said if there was a commander-in-chief of the Dashmesh Regiment it could only be him as he was recognized as the foremost expert in urban warfare. It was he who had trained the Mukti Bahini during the Bangladesh freedom struggle.

Shabeg Singh was dismissed from the army a day before he was due to retire under a special clause which did not even entitle him to a trial. This special clause had never been invoked in the case of any other officer in the history of the Indian Army. Afterwards the matter was handed over to the Central Bureau of Investigation who framed two cases against Shabeg Singh, one that he took a truck in somebody else's name and thereby misused army transport and another saying that he built a house costing Rs 9 lakhs. Shabeg Singh won both cases.

These were not, however, the reasons for his dismissal and for nearly five years after he was thrown out he haunted political circles in Delhi begging to be given a trial. He even approached Giani Zail Singh who was then home minister and said that if a court-martial was not possible then he should be given a civilian trial or even a civilian court of inquiry so that he could clear his name of what he believed were completely false charges. Nothing was done and Shabeg Singh slowly became obsessed with the belief that he had been discriminated against only because he was a Sikh. 'The aim was to deny me my promotion because I was a Sikh. This is how Sikhs are being persecuted in the army.'

Shabeg Singh believed that he had sacrificed the best years of his life for the country. In 12 years of active service he had only taken a six-month break. He fought with honour and distinction in every war and was consumed with bitterness about the 'reward' he had got for his patriotism.

Shabeg Singh was a fanatical Sikh but trimmed his beard and cut his hair to go into Bangladesh disguised as a Muslim. He believed that he had done more to prove his patriotism to India than almost anyone else and that the only reason why he was still a suspect was because he was a Sikh.

After his dishonourable dismissal from the army he turned more and more towards religion and when I met him in the

Akal Rest House, about three weeks before Operation Bluestar, he had been staying at the Golden Temple for three weeks because he had just won the cases that the CBI put up against him and was offering a routine of prayers in thanksgiving.

He would wake up at 3 a.m., have a bath and be ready by 4.30 a.m. for the Palki Sahib Seva when the Guru Granth is carried from the Akal Takht to the Harmandir Sahib. He would then stay on in the gurdwara and do his *Sukhmani Sahib* prayers for another few hours and then return in the evening for the *rehras,* the sunset prayers. In addition, he and his wife, who was seriously ill, used to go every Sunday to the Baba Deep Singh Gurdwara for six hours of meditation and prayers.

Shabeg Singh was a frail, slight man with a long, flowing beard. He looked more like a Sikh priest than a former general. He said that he did not live at the Golden Temple in any permanent sense but came often because his village, Khiala, was only about 16 km away.

On the face of it he looked like an unlikely commander of the Dashmesh Regiment and denied any links with it. He was, in fact, quite amused to hear that his name was being associated with it and said, with a half smile, 'Perhaps it is my fate to have lived through so many wars only to die dishonourably as a terrorist.'

Shabeg Singh made no efforts whatsoever to deny that he believed in Sant Bhindranwale as a leader. He said, 'As far as my relations with Sant Jarnail Singh are concerned, there is nothing to suspect. I've told you that I am a patriot of a finer mould than the prime minister herself. I have met Bhindranwale. There is no doubt about it, and I also feel that there is a strong touch of spiritualism in this person. He is a man who stands by the truth. The government is deliberately terming him a traitor because his brand of politics probably doesn't suit them. But the fact is that there is hardly a Sikh in this world who does not accept him as a leader. I also accept him as a leader. I firmly believe that he is the only Sikh born after Guru Gobind Singh who can get justice for the Sikhs as a community in this country where we have been persecuted ever since Independence and suspected individually and as a community as a whole.'

Apart from Shabeg Singh there were at least two other former generals who were close to Bhindranwale, Major General Jaswant Singh Bhullar and Major General Narinder Singh.

Bhullar, lived in a beautiful house in Chandigarh surrounded by army memorabilia and elegant objects d'art. There were pictures in silver frames, books by Tolstoy and antiques collected from various parts of the country. It was a world so removed from Bhindranwale's that there seemed to be no area on which the two could have found something common. Yet, the former general, in urbane English, expounded the same militant views as the extremists in the Golden Temple and talked about how the Sikhs had always been discriminated against. He admitted that he himself had only become aware of the problem during the Asian Games when he was stopped several times on the way to Delhi and 'humiliated' by Haryana policemen who insisted on searching him even though he had an identity card proving that he was a former general.

Like Shabeg Singh, Jaswant Singh Bhullar looked upon Bhindranwale as a saviour of the Sikhs and defended even his anti-Hindu tirades by saying, 'I have heard most of the speeches and they are most conditional. All that he is trying to say is that if anything is done to the Sikhs settled outside Punjab then don't forget that there could be reprisals against the Hindus living here. So most of the communal things he says are conditional, for instance he said that if my bus is burned – it has happened before when the Guru Granth Sahib was burned (in Chando Kalan)–then if it happens again I will start killing Hindus.'

Major General Narinder Singh also lived in Chandigarh and was as unlikely a supporter of Bhindranwale as Bhullar. He said that he had realized during the Asian Games that Sikhs were not first class citizens. He related stories of how many people he knew had been dragged off buses and humiliated in Haryana only because they were Sikhs. It was after this he decided to go to the ex-servicemen's convention called by Longowal.

Narinder Singh made Trequent trips to the Golden Temple and was often involved in mediating between Longowal and Bhindranwale when differences arose.

Neither Narinder Singh nor Bhullar saw anything wrong in the terrorism that was obviously part of Bhindranwale's philosophy. Narinder Singh said that it was the direct result of police atrocities in Punjab and Bhullar went one step further by saying, 'You see we find that it is the only thing which shakes up the government so we keep quiet about it.'

Men who live by the Stengun are always prepared to die by it one day and as the paramilitary forces started inching closer to the forbidden territory of the Golden Temple, the men inside seemed to become aware that the time had come at last for a final battle. In the month before 6 June there was constant activity inside the extremist camp. Gun battles with the paramilitary forces had by now become a daily occurrence and these necessitated fortifications which seemed to come up overnight.

Slowly the gun battles became longer and more serious and the security forces started setting up positions on rooftops overlooking the temple. The extremists responded by occupying some houses themselves so that the immediate environs of the Golden Temple became a war zone at least ten days before the last battle.

In a funny kind of way the extremists seemed to think that they would succeed in holding off an attack. Somehow, they seemed prepared to fight but not to die. Bhindranwale, himself, gave the impression of being confident till the very end. On 3 June, which was the last day that journalists were allowed in, he was seen personally loading guns and handing them out to his followers.

But after curfew was declared that night and the entire state was closed down for 36 hours it became clear that the army meant business. It was at this stage that a large number of Bhindranwale's men are believed to have escaped through the more obscure exits from the temple. According to some Akalis, who were there till the morning of 6 June, the only people who stayed with Bhindranwale and fought till the very end were the youths who had belonged to the Damdami Taxal.

Whoever they were, the army believes that they were up against at least 1,500 extremists of whom about 500 were the really motivated ones. Some hid in tunnels and manholes and continued fighting till two days after Bhindranwale was killed. A couple of shots were even fired at Zail Singh when he visited the gurdwara on 8 June. On the morning of 6 June, while the fighting continued in the Akal Takht and the Harmandir Sahib, army troops surrounded the Teja Singh Samundari Hall and the Guru Ram Das Serai and took Longowal and Tohra into custody. Bibi Amarjit Kaur was arrested at the same time from a room near the Sikh reference library which was later destroyed in a fire.

Even for the rescued there was a final tragedy when a bomb was thrown into the courtyard of the Ram Das Serai and at least 70 people were killed including the controversial Akali secretary, Gurcharan Singh. Finally, several hours later, the rescued Akalis, pilgrims and SGPC officials were taken out of the gurdwara through a back entrance.

How Harmandir Singh Sandhu happened to be among this lot is a question that people have been asking without finding a satisfactory answer. According to SGPC officials who were there at the time, he was in charge of a gun position on top of the Ram Das Serai and when he saw the army surround the place he came down and mingled with the rest. It is said that he fell at Tohra's feet and begged to be allowed to leave with the rest of them.

Controversy surrounds the death of Amreek Singh, Shabeg Singh and Bhindranwale. One priest, who was hiding near the

Akal Takht, says he saw them on the morning of 6 June. He says that he talked to them and that they told him they had decided to fight on till the very end in view of the extent of damage to the Akal Takht.

After this the fighting continued all day and by the evening of 6 June the army was considering the idea of sending a platoon in after dark with the specific purpose of bringing Bhindranwale out. Around 5 p.m., two police officers were sent in to reconnoitre the area and ran into a couple of injured extremists who told them that Bhindranwale was dead and that his body, along with that of Shabeg Singh and Amreek Singh, was lying near the Akal Takht.

The body had seven bullet holes and was hastily cremated the following day along with hundreds of others which had littered the white marble Parikrama at the end of the battle. So the only member of the inner circle left alive was Harmandir Sandhu. Even Balbir Singh Sandhu is believed to have died in the action although his body was never identified.

Later, when the army captured the Akal Takht they discovered an escape route that they had not known about. Bhindranwale could have escaped if he wanted to. Why did he choose not to? The answer to that question died with him as did the answers to many other questions. In the villages of Punjab, however, they believe he is definitely alive. Some swear on the Granth Sahib that they had dinner with him only the night before. Others say that the reason why they know he is not dead is because he gave his sister some *amrit* one day and told her that only on the day when it turned red should she think that he had died. The *amrit* is still the colour of water so he obviously is alive, they say. The Bhindranwale myth may, by the look of things, prove to be more powerful than the man.

Blood, Sweat and Tears

SHEKHAR GUPTA

25 MAY 1984, AROUND MIDNIGHT

On that breezy summer night in sunburnt south-western Punjab, excitement was palpable in the field headquarters of the 9 Infantry Division of Indian Army. The countdown to the 'H-Hour' had begun and while officers went over the plans and systems one last time, troops did a final, reassuring check of the weapons. In the Operations Room loomed the by now familiar figures of Major General Kuldip Singh ('Bulbul') Brar, General Officer Commanding (GOC) of the Division and Lieutenant General K Sundarji, GOC-in-C, Western Command. Quickly, in his typical clipped tone, Brar laid out his assault plan before Sundarji. And then Sundarji walked across to the 'enemy.'

He was now listening to the strategy of the defenders, yet another of the Indian Army's crack infantry divisions, given the task of defending a ditch-cum-bund from 9 Division's assault. But even as his troops geared up in their defences, there was to be no action for them that night.

For the troops, it was to be, on the face of it, an anti-climax. In a short while, as a terse message landed from higher quarters, Sundarji called off the ambitious 'Exercise Vajraban.' It was time for the troops to end the war-games, and get into a real battle. Mrs Gandhi had finally decided to put an end to the temple terrorism in Punjab.

But to the troops and officers in the field, it was still not clear why such an elaborately planned exercise the 'Vajraban' had been called off so abruptly. They had the impression that they too were required to strengthen security on the Indo-Pakistan border, relieving the Border Security Force (BSF) to tackle insurgency in the countryside, a process which had begun a few days earlier. While the troops packed up and waited in anticipation of the marching orders, the top brass had begun giving final touches to the Operation Bluestar in New Delhi and Simla, where the Western Command headquarters is located. The operation was still a complete secret outside the strategy rooms.

Even to a city familiar with the screech and whine of rifle bullets and the bursts of automatics, the loud bangs on the morning of 5 June came as a rude awakener. People in distant localities could only make wild guesses, but practically everyone in the walled city had an idea of what was happening. The army's recoilless guns and a tank had gone into action as part of a softening up operation to destroy the high-perched firing positions built by Bhindranwale's men in the Golden Temple complex. There were the two eighteenth century towers, called Ramgarhia Bungas, flanking the Guru Ram Das Langar, where Bhindranwale had been holding his daily congregation till recently. Perhaps even more formidable was the gun emplacement atop a concrete water tank behind Teja Singh

Samundari Hall. Men, highly motivated and charged with religious fervour had been manning these, watching practically all possible approaches to the temple complex. The high-rise positions covered every inch of these approaches, up to about a kilometre away. The army knew there would be no approaching the temple without neutralizing these positions. The defenders never expected that the army would hit them with artillery of any kind. A measure of their confidence was the small, saffron pennant fluttering atop one of the *bungas*.

The first shells failed to make much impact. But the army meant business and soon, better ranges and angles were found. As Gurdev Singh, the acting Akali Dal secretary and one of the survivors in the temple precinct recalls, 'Shells hit sandbags and sent them flying, along with men, with flailing limbs. It is only later when the pillboxes and sandbagged firing positions were destroyed that some of the shells went past, without making contact with the targets.' For Major General Brar and his men, the initial workout meant more than merely a softening up operation before the assault. On the contrary, it was expected to stave off the possibility of a frontal assault. The show of firepower, generals felt, would overawe the defenders, besides serving the tactical purpose of clearing the approaches to the temple complex, should an assault become inevitable.

It did. Alongside the shelling and intermittent exchange of automatic fire, those in and around the temple complex were getting used to one more sound, that of the warnings on megaphones, asking the defenders not to be foolhardy and surrender. These made no impact at all. 'Let the army come, we will teach them the lesson of their lifetime,' Bhindranwale often used to say. But his bravado was evidently in the hope that, firstly, the government would be hesitant to use the army, fearing large-scale mutiny by Sikh soldiers and secondly, even if it did, the 'inevitable' revolt by the Sikhs not only in the army but in all civil, paramilitary and police services would help him turn the tables. He had told me confidently just a fortnight before the denouement: 'Even if that Brahmin's daughter (as he often referred to Mrs Gandhi) sends in the army, there is no doubt that the Sikhs will keep out of it. And we are absolutely good enough to deal with the *topi wallas*.' It was the same wishful thinking that obviously added to his men's overconfidence.

But on this day, they were in for a rude surprise. Commandants of four of the six assault battalions were Sikhs, two of the three commanding generals, Divisionsal Commander Brar and Western Command Chief of Staff Ranjit Singh Dayal, were Sikhs. And the battalion that launched the first assault, the 10 Guards, was a mixed unit containing a generous sprinkling of Sikhs. But the same bravura had left the thousand-odd men to the right of the *bungas* untouched. Most of these consisted of Akali Dal and SGPC officials and workers, besides over 500 pilgrims who had come in on 3 June, the martyrdom day of Guru Arjun Dev. Yet though they all took the warnings seriously there was no getting away without risking one's life as bullets flew all over. Only 117, including a large number of labourers engaged by the SGPC, took the risk of walking out and surrendering to the army. As subsequent events proved, they are the ones who weighed the odds correctly. Of those who chose to stay inside, no less than half never came out and many ended up maimed for life.

'One-five, infantry suffering heavy casualties. One-five, infantry suffering heavy casualties. Tank support imperative and necessary,' crackled the voice on the wireless set as the generals and staff paced about impatiently, following the course of the battle ensconced in a high-rise building with an overview of the complex. Only about an hour earlier, they had taken the painful step of launching the infantry to free the temple complex of its sticky, gritty occupants. The unit chosen to lead the assault was 10 Guards, known for decades for its fierce, do-or-die reputation. On this evening of 6 June it was being tested severely.

Four years back the compound in front of the Golden Temple's main entrance used to be a wide, wind-swept patio, forming a kind of an oasis in the congested walled city. But the first fall-out of the Akali agitation that began three-and-a-half years ago had been the encroachment of structures facing the entrance that rapidly devoured the open space. A tall wall barred part of it. The new stalls for keeping pilgrims's shoes too were constructed outside the temple complex, reducing the space further, limiting the approach to a fairly narrow passage to the entrance. And it was more than effectively guarded by pillboxes along the parapet of the Parikrama (circumambulation), on the clocktower, on the main entrance gate and, most effective of all, on the terrace and from inside the rooms of Hotel Temple View, formerly a favourite with the pilgrims and which had some time back been occupied by the militants as part of their strategy to set up watch-posts along the periphery of the temple. Similarly, the ancient Brahm Buta Akhara overlooking the narrow entrance to the Serais' side was a militant stronghold. Before the main assault, the army wanted the two buildings cleared and decided to use the jawans of the CRPF and BSF instead. After a brief firefight, the CRPF was able to clear the Akhara early in the evening. Hotel Temple View posed more problems as militants fought out and the BSF commandos could overcome resistance only after lobbing grenades in some of the top floor rooms. The BSF commandos suffered two casualties in the process.

The forward posts removed, the way was more or less clear for the Guardsmen who were expected to be joined in from the Serais' side by men of 26 Madras and a company of Kumaonis. The generals were still hopeful of a quick capitulation. As an officer recalled later, the optimism stemmed from the fact that while the Guardsmen spilled into the side facing the temple and the Akal Takht, followed by men of the 7 Garhwal from the gate facing the main entrance, the collective assault would prove too daunting for the defenders who would surrender, avoiding bloodshed. But two factors made it a futile hope. One, that the defenders were not rational or calculating, weighing their risks. Second, the operation did not exactly go as planned and the troops failed to spill into the Parikrama at the same time, thus unable to surprise the extremists with a sudden, massive invasion. On the other hand, the militants just had the Guards to deal with and the troops took the brunt of firing from all three sides.

The Guardsmen had slipped in, hugging the outer periphery, and, thus escaping the initial fire from the pillboxes along the parapets that covered the approaches but unable to do much about the intruders walking right beneath. However the secure feeling was momentary as the first company, led by Captain Jasbir Singh Raina, a Sikh, broke in. A body of men, also led by a Sikh junior commissioned officer (JCO), also set about the task of clearing the militant-infested rooms along the Parikrama. But the Guards battalion, led by Lt Col Israr Khan had run into more than it had expected. Even the initial volley fired by the militants felled nearly a score of Guardsmen, including Captain Raina. The intensity of fighting is best described in the words of an officer from one of the paramilitary forces who happened to be leading a picket in the nearby Katra Ahluwalia. 'I will never forget that scene,' he said, adding, 'when the troops first went in one of my colleagues had been joking with the Army Medical Corps men accompanying the two ambulances parked at the edge of the market, facing the temple. He had been telling them how futile was their wait going to be as the militants were not likely to put up a fight. And how we were proved wrong. Within minutes we found nine bodies lying there and the men in the ambulances had more than a handful.'

But the Guardsmen were not the ones to be daunted by casualties. Noticing that the militants, obviously following Shabeg Singh's advice, had sited machine guns 23 cm above the ground along the Parikrama, the army officers quickly instructed the troops to refrain from crawling. 'It was difficult, but the only tactics we could possibly have used,' recalled an officer, describing how troops were told to use for cover the rather slender marble pillars along the Parikrama, and spring out whenever there was a momentary lull in machine gun fire to lob a grenade inside a room. But that did not solve the problem, for, as the troops discovered later, Shabeg Singh had thick walls built, dividing each room into several sections. Consequently, often even when a grenade burst it cleared out only one section of the room while the extremists hiding in the rest did a bloody kamikaze act with approaching jawans, shooting, though they knew they would not get away.

But even as the troops pressed on, they were being badgered by the generals to do more, and quickly. While the ground floor of the Parikrama itself was taking time, the generals were desperate that the first floor parapet positions were also cleared out first as these were threatening the troops coming in from other sides. The troops made a mad rush for the staircase at each end of the Parikrama. But Shabeg had not earned his reputation of a wily, doughty commander in the army for nothing. He had anticipated just this and the sprinting troops ran headlong into automatic fire from men who sprang out of the manholes, strategically situated at the foot of each staircase. With no time to lose, the commanders ordered the troops to throw assault ladders and get up on the parapet.

As the Guardsmen fought on, troops of the Madras, Kumaon and Garhwal Regiments were facing their own problems. The Madras battalion, commanded by Lt Col Panikkar, had not been able to join up with the Guards at the expected time because of the extraordinary strength of the steel gate guarding the entrance from the serais' side. A Vijayanta tank had to be used as a battering ram to break it open. Further, as soon as they entered the complex, the 26 Madras troops encountered fire from militants hiding in the *piao* (water stall) in front of Guru Ram Das Serai and immediately suffered casualties. By the time they were neutralized, it was time for a company of Kumaoni troops to move into the Parikrama from the same entrance. In the dark, as confusion reigned, the troops of the two units got mixed on the steps. Inevitably, the officers had to go through the painful process of first separating their respective troops before joining battle.

Around this time, jawans of 7 Garhwal, a unit drawn from the reserves of the 15 Infantry Division posted at Amritsar and not directly participating in the action, came in from the gate facing the main entrance. Firing a recoilless gun in confined space, two of their jawans died of the back-flash.

This brought into the arena Brigadier (now Major General) A.K. Diwan (nicknamed Cheeky), then the deputy GOC of 15 Infantry Division who had initially come in to coordinate the transfer of his unit's troops to the field of action but now stepped in to see what had gone wrong. Inexorably, he was drawn into action which was to prove even more fierce than the fight with the Chinese for Chushul in 1962 when, as a young Captain, Diwan had led a contingent of tanks of the 20 Lancers Regiment of Armoured Corps. The feat of taking and effectively using tanks at some of the highest altitudes in the history of modern warfare had brought him a Vir Chakra. On the night of 5 June, however, he was at the head of not tanks but infantrymen who were not sure which side the enemy was and on which their own troops. The danger of jawans getting caught in fellow units' crossfire was real and officers in the Parikrama recall the silhouetted figure of Diwan blinking a torch and shouting at the men of Madras and Kumaon regiments, 'Don't shoot, I am the Deputy GOC.' Diwan's providential arrival on the scene was to have decisive impact on the situation as it helped control the confusion with jawans from various units crammed on the Parikrama floor. With the infantry busy clearing up the Parikrama, the task of 'contacting' the Akal Takht was left to the highly-trained commandos of Special Frontier Force (SFF), the secret outfit run by the RAW at

Chakrata near Mussoorie. Originally the installation, also called 'Establishment 22,' had been set up after the 1962 Indo-China War with American help to train Dalai Lama's followers in guerrilla warfare to carry out hit-and-run raids against the Chinese garrisons in Tibet. With the passage of time and change in the geo-political situation, the Establishment had lost its original relevance. But it is here now that the government maintains its best-equipped and trained commando outfit, officered mainly by men drawn from the parachute and commando units of the army. The SFF commandos had been the only ones to have had the opportunity to practise the raid on a fairly accurate mock-up of the temple complex at Chakrata and Sarsawa near Saharanpur in Uttar Pradesh. It was now the same men, commanded by Lt Col Chowdhury and dressed in their usual black dungarees and bulletproof vests, trying to head stealthily for the Akal Takht from the flanks, hoping to deliver a quick coup de grace. But that was not to be as Shabeg and his men had the approaches well covered. With casualties mounting, the commandos found progress impossible and advised 'one-five,' the code for the command post to use tanks. The commanders decided to first use the old-fashioned foot soldiers instead.

With the benefit of hindsight it is often asked now why the commandos did not try to break into the Akal Takht through one of the back lanes or through one of the adjoining rooftops. The logic is that a frontal assault without any element of surprise stands in inherent contradiction of commando warfare. But officers involved in the action said the possibility had been examined earlier, but given up since most of the buildings behind the Akal Takht were found to be occupied and fortified by Bhindranwale's men. The situation had obviously changed for the worse since April 1984 when the commandos had first begun making reconnaissance visits in CRPF uniforms. It was also because of this increasing fortification and rapid increase in militants' qualitative and quantitative armed strength that the government had given up its initial plan of a purely commando assault in the temple complex in April. According to the first plan, drafted in longhand by Shiva Swarup, Director-General of the CRPF, a joint force of commandos drawn in from all paramilitary forces, including the BSF and Indo-Tibetan Border Police (ITBP), was to prise out the militants after breaking in through a gap in the Parikrama wall, to be blasted with explosives. The scheme demanded that the army release some armoured personnel carriers and 84 mm, shoulder-fired Carl Gustav guns. One of the reasons the scheme was not pursued seriously was the army's refusal to part with the equipment. Later, however, a less practical plan was rehearsed, involving about 300 SFF commandos. This was given up as rehearsals threw up weaknesses and Bhindranwale fortified himself better inside the Akal Takht. Even that night, it was not a task for the commandos any more.

Alongside, in the commanders' quest for a relatively bloodless operation, attempts were being made to toss 'CS' gas canisters into the Akal Takht. Only slightly stronger than the tear-gas that the police use, the 'CS' gas grenades are a lot milder than the stun grenades used by Britain's famed Special Air Service. Yet, if aimed correctly, these would have served the army's purpose of at least leaving the defenders confused and with visions blurred and while they tried to recover, the Akal Takht could have been taken. But even this did not work. Heavily sandbagged windows and entrances left no gaps through which grenades could be lobbed in even when the commandos got perilously close to the Akal Takht. Soon, however, the army found the cost of continuing the operation prohibitive. As an officer recalls, these grenades can be lobbed only at close range and to get that close in that situation amounted to committing suicide. The whole marble square between the Akal Takht and the Darshani Deori was covered with machine guns, some of them peeping most menacingly out of battlements cut in the thick marble wall of the Akal Takht building, less than half a metre above ground. This was Shabeg Singh's killing ground. As the marble floor left jawans devoid of any cover whatsoever, the militants' combination of grazing and plunging fire, sweeping every bit of the area, made any approach impossible.

It was in such a situation that the foot-soldiers were made to launch assault after assault. The Kumaonis led by Major Mishra, almost made it to the building's entrance, but with disastrous consequences. A murderous volley of fire cut down the assault team, leaving Major Mishra and at least seven other ranks dead. Even as the bodies lay sprawled in front of the marble citadel, the commandant of the Madras Battalion, asked to follow up the attack, requested for volunteers. Led by a young captain, the dare-devil bunch of ten volunteers leapt across and, with unparalelled courage, pressed on despite fire to enter the Akal Takht building, the first and the only troops to succeed in doing so while resistance was still on. But to their misfortune, the section ran headlong into about 30 militants who were running down the narrow staircase. In the shootout that ensued in the confined space, only the most fortunate on either side could have survived. Of the troops, six died, two crawled back, wounded, and one, a JCO, lay wounded in the passage with the captain trying to bring him back. For nearly half an hour, as the officer tried desperately to reach his wounded comrade in the dark, the commanders waiting outside presumed he had fallen too. Finally, finding it impossible to trace his wounded JCO in the dark in the heap of dead and wounded men and amid heavy fire, the officer crawled back. At this stage, the futility of launching frontal infantry attacks was clear to the commanders. As one of them later said, a whole division of troops would have to be sent in against such well-planned and built defences, manned by people with determination. It was time to go for drastic measures.

Meanwhile, it was not only in front of the Akal Takht that troops were dying. The Parikrama was covered by deadly snipers hiding in the Harmandir Sahib, shooting at whoever stirred out in the open. Officers and men survived jumping from one marble pillar to another. Later, the heavily chipped pillars bore ample evidence of the fire which could, in all probability, have come in only from the temple. But that was one fire the troops were prohibited to return and officers recall situations of near insubordination as they tried to prevent their men from firing back. In the last-minute address to the troops before the assault, Brar had said: 'In no circumstances are you to fire at the temple. I know this amounts to sending somebody to the boxing ring with one hand tied behind his back. But here, this will have to be done.' The orders to officers were to hand out summary punishment, even dismissal to anyone violating this order and it is only because of this that the temple still stood after the operation more or less intact, barring some bullet marks that could have resulted from strays in the heavy crossfire. Among those who fell to the snipers hiding in the temple was Lieutenant Ram Prakash Ruparia of the 26 Madras who caught a bullet in the neck on June 6 as he tried to climb down from the first floor of Parikrama to bring water for his troops lying prone for hours under a withering sun. Ruparia died three days later in the field hospital and, in a touch of brutal irony, his body was sent to his native village in Haryana on 10 June, his birthday. 'You let us down, Ram Prakash,' said his grief-stricken father repeatedly. 'We had always thought it will take at least 20 to 25 bullets to kill Ram Prakash. And here, see, you could not survive one.' For the officers and men of Madras Regiment this was the sad end of a simple, courageous and extremely popular officer, often called 'Robert Prince Ruparia,' his modified, anglicized name a tribute to his rustic simplicity. Ruparia's men did not fire back at the temple.

Initially, the commanders' concept of drastic measures was the use of wheeled, 'Scot' armoured personnel carriers (APCs) that were supposed to take troops safely into the vicinity of the Akal Takht. A number of APCs of a mechanized infantry unit were kept outside the temple gate for such a contingency. But as one was brought in, it ran into problems. The fairly high marble steps at the entrance facing the serais made it a perilous drive in for the APCs. A tank was thus used to crush the marble steps,one at a time and reversing, to ensure that it did not roll down, blocking the only safe passage available for the entry of tanks into the Parikrama. But there was yet another surprise in store for the troops as the militants unleashed a surprise weapon, a 40 mm, Chinese-made RPG-7 and one of the first shots bored through the side of the lead APC, wounding Captain Jagdev Singh, in command. The immobilized vehicle was now a sitting duck and the commanders ordered the troops to abandon it. It was in that process that the driver, while alighting, was shot in the eye and killed.

The generals had by now begun to realise that they had miscalculated the determination, firepower and the skill of the defenders and that could no longer delay the inevitable, the use of tanks. The commandant of the commando unit had even initially asked for the use of armour and many other officers on the ground also held the same view, but the top brass was hesitant for valid reasons. Firstly, the use of tanks for shelling would certainly cause substantial damage to the Akal Takht building. Second, even if the main gun was not used, the tank tracks were bound to damage parts of the marble floor of the Parikrama. It was for that reason that they had refrained from using the tracked, sturdy, Soviet-made BMP-I, a heavily armed infantry combat vehicle (ICV). Instead they had used Scot APCs with wheels. Such an APC was more vulnerable to a barrage of sustained, intense fire. But they were running out of time and patience. Sunrise was not very far away and the commanders reckoned that, once there was light, survival would become impossible for each one of the nearly 800 troops still inside the Parikrama. Besides, reports coming in from villages surrounding Amritsar were consistently alarming, with the army and police having a tough time dealing with mobs of angry Sikhs marching towards Amritsar to 'save the Harmandir Sahib.' All along the day on 5 June, helicopter reconnaissance patrols had been spotting mob formations all over the district. One mob that got perilously close to Amritsar town in the direction of the Raja Sansi Airport was intercepted in the nick of time by a column of jawans who overcame it only with the use of intense automatic fire. Much of it was, however, directed at the mob's flanks, killing just eight persons.

Similarly large mobs had been gathering near the milk village of Verka and at Golwad near Jhabal, about 25 km from Amritsar, under the leadership of a preacher Baba Bidhi Chand. With every passing hour army and police officers had been reporting an increase in the intensity of mob fury. As an officer later said, 'Each successive mob that we encountered was more furious and required use of greater force. Now there is a limit to which you can use force against a crowd. After all, you can't use artillery against them and kill hundreds of people.' In retrospect, the marching of mobs was one pre-planned Bhindranwale operation that failed to come off. For months since he began fearing a police entry into the temple complex his speeches ended with exhortations like: 'They say they will send police into the Harmandir Sahib. Let them do so. Many of you come and ask me, "what will happen to you in that case?" Don't worry about us. We will take care. But believe me, once Harmandir Sahib is attacked, there will be no future left for the Sikhs outside. You all will be butchered. So the moment you get the first inkling of an attack take up arms and start taking revenge.' In a series of tell-tale euphemisms that would follow, the hint always was that the revenge was killing of Hindus. On 3 June, just while the army was sealing the trap around his bastion, he had told me: 'We can hold them off for long enough here. But the real job will have to be done by the Sikhs all over the world. My message to them would be, *apne apne haath se apna kaaj sanwariye* (use your own hands to do what is good for you).'

The exhortation taken out of the holy Sikh scriptures later became the militants' code-word to begin slaughtering Hindus and to march to the Golden Temple as soon as the siege began, and it had apparently gone around even on the morning of 3 June, hours before the first columns of the army moved in. On that quiet morning, India Today photo editor Raghu Rai and I had gone to the small *mandi*-town of Rayya, nearly 40 km from Amritsar, to look at the impact of the Akali call to blockade the transport of wheat at the *mandis*. On the way back, we decided to take a detour via the village of Nagoke, about 20 km from the Grand Trunk Road. Nagoke has been the cradle of militancy and Kulwant Singh Nagoke, one of the first Bhindranwale men to have died at the hands of the police, hailed from here. My idea was to visit his place as part of a continuing study of the phenomenon of extremism. But the atmosphere in his house was tense, with his widow doing all the talking and a bunch of eight young men keeping absolutely quiet. The truth dawned on us as we were leaving. One of the youths took me aside and dropped the bombshell, saying: 'I have seen you with Santji (Bhindranwale). So we feel sorry for you. Please run away as soon as you can. Word has gone round to kill all the pandits (Bhindranwale's favourite expression to describe all Hindus). No one will even bother to stop your car, they will just shoot. And I am afraid I cannot help you beyond the boundaries of this village.' And then he added, as an afterthought, '*Hun kam shuru ho giya hai* (now the campaign has begun).'

Thus, while the commanders battled with the option of sending in the tanks, the 'campaign' had been on for over 60 hours and sheer providence had so far prevented a large-scale massacre. While the local authorities were getting increasingly worried, pressure had been mounting from Delhi as well to achieve results quickly as curfew could not be maintained for an indefinite period and a relaxation was unavoidable the following day.

Initially, the idea of Generals Sundarji, Dyal and Brar was to use tanks only for giving armoured cover to the advancing infantry while giving the militant battlements a workout with its turret machine gun at close range. To break the will of the defenders, the bigger bangs were to be provided by the 3.7 inch howitzer, which fires at fairly close ranges horizontally, unlike the modern artillery pieces that fire only at a trajectory, which renders their use tricky at short ranges and in confined spaces where half a metre here and there could make all the difference between victory and disaster. An artillery colonel – a specialist observation post flier – was instructed to haul a howtizer up on a rooftop overlooking the Akal Takht. The choice initially fell on the Punjab National Bank building. Civilians from nearby houses helped the gunners haul up the howitzer with ropes. But after repeated attempts failed, another building nearby was chosen. The stage was now set for the fire assault on the Akal Takht building.

Initially, the howitzer fired only smoke shells to find the target. But the real fireworks followed shortly afterwards and these were responsible for the damage to the domes of the Akal Takht. Yet, this failed to have the desired effect quickly enough and, with first light just a little over an hour away, the tank-men received the clearance to open up with the main, 105-mm gun. Over 80 shells were fired and these accounted for the whole front facade of the Akal Takht and pillars. To begin with, as the tank-men failed to distinguish the Darshani Deori from the Akal Takht, thanks to its peculiar location in straight line with the latter, a few shells were misdirected. These caused the destruction to the small Darshani Deori domes and also part of the Toshakhana where chandni, the bejewelled canopy gifted to the temple by Maharaja Ranjit Singh, was burnt. Some shells – it is difficult to say whether from the tanks or howitzer – also fell in the congested localities behind the Akal Takht, flattening scores of houses. One of the high-explosive shells in fact strayed and landed across the town, over 5 km away, inside Shahid Nagar, the officers' residential colony in the cantonment, wounding an unsuspecting jawan. Odd misses apart, the guns did their job effectively and as dawn broke on 6 June, the only resistance in the temple complex came from the snipers. The main defences of the Akal Takht had been 'neutralized'.

The troops were, however, still not sure about the fate of Bhindranwale and his key associates like Shabeg Singh, Bhai Amreek Singh and Thara Singh and since intermittent fire continued from the Akal Takht, no attempt was still made to storm it physically.

The first indications of a capitulation came around 11 a.m. Officers recall the strange spectacle of about 25 militants rushing out of the building, firing at random and running straight into death as troops opened up in all their pent-up fury. A few threw away their weapons and managed to jump into the Amrit Sarovar, the holy tank around the temple, in sheer desperation. Jawans picked them out quickly. The generals guessed that the mad dash was an indication that Bhindranwale was either dead or wounded or had, confirming their worst fears, escaped. Yet the situation was considered reassuring enough to allow the district authorities to order a two-hour relaxation in curfew in the afternoon.

And how Amritsar came to life in just those two hours! No vehicles were allowed; there was thus a procession of thousands of men on all roads, out shopping for food, vegetables and medicines. Rotting, week-old *dussehri* mangoes sold for Rs 12 a kg. There were long queues even in front of a group of shops selling fodder for cattle – so acute had fodder shortage been during the curfew that, with restrictions on movement making it impossible for them to take their cattle out for grazing, many in Amritsar had taken the painful decision of leaving their cattle astray, to fend for themselves. But even in such bleak times, the Punjabi sense of enterprise was visible all over, nothing representing it more effectively than the figure of a Sikh youth with polythene shopping bags slung over his shoulders, skating merrily past The Mall, beating the ban on plying vehicles, even bicycles.

Deeper inside the walled city, the atmosphere was different as crowds welled to have a closer look at the exteriors of the temple complex, a persistent throng also hung around the brick-red *Kotwali* building, barely 400 m from the temple, where the army had been bringing in the captured militants. But the crowds and even police officers present at the *kotwali* were not as keenly interested in the prisoners as in the two private trucks parked outside, loaded with bodies of people killed inside the temple complex. The policemen and municipal sweepers, entrusted with the task of clearing the bodies, had not done it with any respect to the dead. Limbs of the dead still hung outside the sides of the vehicles and blood seeped out of the crevices in the truck. In the later stages of the operation, however, as scores of bodies hidden inside rooms and under the debris rotted, stank and even grew maggots, the army had a tough time persuading even the municipal workers to pick them. Through sheer intimidation they succeeded in bringing a bunch of sweepers from Islamabad, a predominantly Dalit locality. But officers recall that a number of them fainted after picking just a body or two. As a major concession now, the civil and military police officers supervising the 'scavenging' allowed the workers to remove the dead men's belongings as compensation. Later when even that did not work, the army's universally accepted currency, rum, was used in generous measure.

The brief, two hour reprieve from curfew brought for the onlookers other shocks too. There was, for example, the gory sight of about a dozen suspected militants caught from the Akal Takht, being pushed by jawans towards the kotwali in spite of their injuries and beaten up rudely in the kotwali compound.

Immediately afterwards, they were lined up in the verandah, facing a light machine gun, while a Sikh officer questioned them. Each bit of information they revealed was passed on to the troops to be conveyed to the officers still battling inside. The machine gun never boomed though wild rumours later talked of suspected militants having been machine gunned by the dozen in the *kotwali* verandah.

Closer to the temple, surprises were of the other variety. The whole road was lined up on both sides with tanks, APCs, recoilless guns and jawans carrying Carl Gustav guns and LMGs besides the usual self-loading rifles and carbines. Their faces showed fatigue and anger. There were dozens showing dressings and pieces of adhesive plaster on minor wounds. But on the road leading out of the serais, facing the Brahm Buta Akhara, there were two trucks, each carrying bodies of six troops on bunks along the sides. At least two of the bodies I was able to look at closely still showed fresh beads of perspiration, indicating that the jawạns could not have died very long ago. While the troops still maintained their composure to some degree, the CRPF men guarding the street were quite obviously full of anger. There was a young sub-inspector with bandages all over his face and lips, who beat up any Sikh found in saffron turban, considered to be a sign of protest. Also, the communal schism could not have been clearer in the heart of the city. Scores of people were roaming on the road, offering chapattis, pickle, dal and lassi to the jawans. Not one of them was a Sikh. In a tell-tale gesture shortly afterwards, the army authorities forbade the troops from accepting eatables from any civilian as it could lead to their getting a biased image. An officer even went around confiscating utensils to discourage the do-gooders.

Inside the temple, however, it was business as usual despite the relaxation in curfew, and outside one could still hear the sounds of gunfire, so close it made you wish you could hide. It was only much later in the day that a wounded *sevadar* crawled out of the Akal Takht building and informed the army that while Bhindranwale and Amreek Singh had died, Shabeg Singh lay wounded. The army now entered the ruins of the building, snuffed out the challenge from a handful of survivors who, while keeping the troops engaged, had been hurling arms and valuables into the deep well behind the Akal Takht, perhaps for use in future – it was all fished out later by divers requisitioned from the navy. The body of Bhindranwale was found in a heap of about 40 corpses near the Akal Takht basement. Shabeg and Amreek were not very far away, though it took the officers a little time recognising the former major general's body. In spite of the destruction that they had initially planned to avoid, the officers heaved a sigh of relief. The main part of Operation Metal, meant to snuff out militants inside the Golden Temple complex, was now over, even if at an enormous cost. Officers recall how the whole building smelt of cordite and gunpowder. The floor in some rooms inside the Akal Takht was covered with ankle deep heap of spent cartridges. Senior officers, in fact, wondered how the militants had been able to fire so much during the night. As one of them said, 'Automatic fire is all right, but you can't do it all the time. Your weapons develop problem and, if nothing else, the barrels melt unless you give adequate pauses between bursts.' The frequency with which the militants fired could have earned an armyman a severe reprimand for misusing weapons. A number of militants, officers recall, had deep blue bruises on the shoulders, a clear indication of their tenacity in defence. They may have been short on rationalism, but motivation was obviously around in abundant supply, as was evident from the efforts some of the arrested militants made to touch the dead Bhindranwale's feet, lying on display on slabs of ice near the main entrance.

But while the spotlight was on the Akal Takht, another important aspect of the operation was being enacted in the serais, flanking the temple complex. One of the first steps in the operation had been to seal off the serais from the temple, neutralize all opposition and bring out safely the leaders of the moderate group of the Akali Dal including its president and morcha 'dictator' Sant Harchand Singh Longowal, SGPC president Gurcharan Singh Tohra, Akali Dal's official spokesman Balwant Singh Ramoowalia and scores of other important functionaries. In the beginning it all seemed to be going nicely as Major Palta, commanding the company of Kumaonis in the serai area, radioed a message back to the command post saying that he was able to progress without much opposition.

And then, suddenly, all hell broke loose as the Kumaonis came under a heavy fusilade of fire and an alarmed Major Palta informed 'one-five' of casualties on his side. But in spite of the fire-fight, the troops had been able to reach the ground floor room in Teja Singh Samundari Hall, the headquarters of the SGPC, where Longowal, Tohra, Ramoowalia and other leaders were sitting in quiet wait. Along with them, the troops found a surprise catch, the Akhand Kirtani Jatha leader Amarjit Kaur who was believed to have been behind the killings of Nirankaris to avenge the death of her husband Fauja Singh, killed at the head of a Sikh procession during the Nirankari congregation at Amritsar on 13 April 1978. The armymen asked the Akalis to stay put till APCs could be arranged to transport them safely outside. Yet, in the process, a band of killers sent in by Bhindranwale succeeded in throwing grenades and firing long automatic bursts, killing a number of pilgrims and former Akali Dal secretary Gurcharan Singh who had been on top of Bhindranwale's hit list. 'That Gurcharan, he will not live very long. If that *shanti da doot* (messenger of peace, Bhindranwale's sarcastic way of addressing Longowal) does not hand him over to us, we will make sure he is put on the train (a very inept translation for his Punjabi '*gaddi chadha devange*'),' Bhindranwale used to tell his followers after the murder of his key associate Surinder Singh Sodhi, for which he blamed Gurcharan Singh. Also killed alongside was SGPC member Bagga Singh, who had been openly accusing Bhindranwale of behaving like a Guru. In fact, to ridicule Bhindranwale, he had begun tying his turban like him and also carried around a stainless-steel arrow to make the mimicry perfect.

But the assassinations triggered off a process, much of which still remains unexplained. According to one explanation, some members of the assassination squad locked themselves in some of the rooms in the serai area where hundreds of pilgrims had been hiding out of sheer panic. As jawans approached the rooms, they were fired at, resulting in casualties. At this stage, since the speedy neutralisation of the serais was imperative to the success of the Operation, the jawans decided to just lob grenades. 'It was a war-like situation where people were getting killed on all sides. There really was no time or scope for niceties any more,' said a junior officer there. This, coupled with the indiscriminate lobbing of grenades by the militant hit squad earlier, accounted for most of the nearly 500 innocent civilians' death. In the words of Jagir Singh, a youngster who survived the mayhem and spoke to me at Amritsar's Shahid Baba Deep Singh gurdwara on the day of his release by the army authorities after screening: 'There was utter confusion as bombs burst and bullets flew all over. Along with nearly a dozen others, I just locked myself inside one of the rooms of Guru Ram Das Serai. After a while, we heard bombs blasting in nearby rooms and the whole world seemed to shake. Somehow, our room was completely ignored. We were all miserable with thirst, yet no one had the courage to open the door. The room stank, with no other place for people to answer the call of nature. By next morning, when the jawans knocked at our door, four of us had died of thirst and exhaustion. I was half-dead. I only remember the armymen smashing a ventilator open, and then an officer asking troops to take positions while we unlocked the door. The rest was not too bad as the army took us away to the prison camp in the Central School compound in the cantonment. The only problem was that, occasionally, the odd jawan would rough up one of us, shouting "*Pakistani ki aulad* (offspring of a

Pakistan)".' Presumably, the jawans' ire resulted from the discovery of circumcised men among those fighting at the Akal Takht and nearly 40 other Muslims who, nevertheless, claimed to be no more than Bangladeshi labourers and gave the address of a clump of villages in Bihar's Bhagalpur district.

Anyway, in the melee that ensued in the serais, causing large-scale deaths of pilgrims, the Kumaonis lost their commander, Major Palta. According to survivors' accounts, he was shot by Anokh Singh, one of the prominent members of the anti-Bhindranwale Babbar Khalsa. Incidentally, the Babbars' proximity with Longowal was not a matter of conjecture. On the day the army first moved in around the temple, the Babbar chief, Sukhdev Singh, was ensconced in a long discussion with Longowal, who was embarrassed when I walked in, on 3 June afternoon. In retrospect, however, the Babbars proved to be the shrewdest of all. Till the army came in, they were the ones continuously provoking the paramilitary forces around the temple, with whom they intermittently exchanged fire. Today, barring the few who died on top of the water tank, the rest of the group, nearly 30-40 strong, escaped breaking a wall behind the Guru Nanak Niwas and using a small passage leading to the narrow bylanes behind. The army, apparently, was unaware of this. Again, in retrospect, from the army's point of view, it was extremely fortunate that the more prominent militant leaders were not on this side of the temple, or the whole Operation would have been rendered futile. The scale of the escape is obvious from the fact that, along with the Babbars and the members of pro-Bhindranwale Akal Federation, led by Bhai Kanwar Singh, nearly 150 pilgrims and SGPC employees also escaped using the passage. An SGPC employee recalled cynically: 'The passage was open and it was now a question of exposing your back to the fire for a moment and rushing out. Many of us did that and there we saw on the run, dozens of those who had taken the so-called holy oath of defending the temple to death. Here they were, throwing away their guns and holsters and running for dear lives.' But the escape attempts which some of the militants made a week later were less than cowardly. Two of them, Kuljinder Singh and Harjinder Singh, wounded in action, escaped from the Sri Guru Teg Bahadur Hospital and have not been traced so far. Even more daring, on 7 June, just a day after the main operation, a large number of militants held near Panther Institute in the cantonment managed to snatch the carbine of a lieutenant on duty and tried to make a break. Alarmed, the jawans opened fire, killing nine militants. In the confusion, a number of jawans erecting a barbed wire fence round the camp were also trapped in the crossfire. Four of them died.

While the army had anticipated casualties in the battle for the Akal Takht, the sudden flare-up in the serai area had been rather unexpected. With the benefit of hindsight, it is now said that more of the pilgrims could have been rescued if the army had given long enough period of warning before the main invasion. But the army's explanation was that not many pilgrims were inclined to come out anyway because of the firing by the militants. The latter even fired at Longowal, Tohra and others, who had to be taken out in APCs. Tohra, incidentally, collapsed due to exhaustion while coming out of the vehicle. Besides, the army officers argued that it was incorrect to say that the pilgrims could not have heard the warnings because of the general noise and commotion. They pointed out that on the evening of 5 June, even the militants had asked for a 30-minute ceasefire to make up their minds on surrender. But later they resumed firing on their own. The short reprieve had probably been utilized to strengthen a fortification or perhaps for moving an important weapon from one place to another.

Even with the capitulation of the Akal Takht and neutralization of the resistance from the serais, there was no relief for the army commanders. The ultimate objective, the Golden Temple, was still holding out. 'Boxing with one hand tied behind their backs,' the jawans watched helpless as a small band of militants kept firing from the temple and frustrated their repeated attempts to break in without firing. In the meantime, the generals got worried by the information given by the captives that the militants had put charges around the temple and were planning to blow it up. Immediately, the frogmen of 1 Paracommando Battalion were ordered to swim across the Sarovar to defuse the explosives. But snipers were ready for them and inflicted some casualties. Later, it turned out to be a false alarm as explosives' experts scanned the temple after the defenders surrendered. Army officers recalled that each one of the 22 who had surrendered in the temple was desperate to go to the toilet as they had had no place to ease themselves in the temple for over two days. Initially, the commanders deployed a band of infantry-men to occupy the temple. Later in the evening, the task was handed over to 20 Sikh jawans and a JCO drawn from the Engineers Battalion involved in the Operation. But even now, if someone expected an end to the fighting, the optimism was soon to be dashed.

Odd bands of survivors, living on a diet of parched gram, *shakarpara* and biscuits, provided to each one in ample measure, besides buffer stocks held in strategic corners of the complex, continued to put up resistance. They hid in ruined buildings, under debris inside small tunnels linking buildings and manholes to harass the troops with repeated sniper attacks. Some of these were also made from the numerous windows in the Ramgarhia Bunga which had to be ultimately scanned and cleared by the 1 Paracommando troops. But greater problems were in store elsewhere. Next to the Akal Takht, a lone sniper continued to hold out in a building, ignoring repeated army entreaties to surrender. Troops had to lob grenades to kill him, but the blasts also blew up a stock of 60 LPG cylinders stored inside the buildings setting off a real blaze. Similarly, a lone sniper with just a .303 rifle continued to fire from a window under the Sikh library along the Parikrama. Grenades hurled to kill him set the library on fire which, fanned by a strong breeze, accounted for hundreds of rare manuscripts and valuable scriptures before the firefighters could come in. In fact, anticipating such a situation, the army had already brought in a brigadier who specialized in putting out fires. But snipers and breeze made his task difficult. Yet another fire broke out in the Teja Singh Samundari Hall as a grenade hit a car parked in its compound. The car apparently had a full tank.

Fires apart, the sniper fire on 7 and 8 June caused the army even more discomfiture than the straightforward assault on the Akal Takht. Some of the accounts were stranger than fiction. The Madras Regiment jawans decided to be kind to an old woman who had come out of a room crying, begging for water. As the jawans got up to help they were cut down by a volley of fire from another woman hiding behind. Troops also recalled in awe the sight of the body of an old woman next to an LMG, her right hand all but severed at the wrist. But in the series of wild incidents the most gruesome was enacted near the Bungas. Captain Rampal of the Army Medical Corps was casually roaming about, looking for any wounded needing first aid as a bunch of militants sprang out of the small, tunnel-like structure linking the basement of the Bunga to a structure next to the Parikrama. He was kidnapped, along with a member of his paramedical staff. But the armymen were able to raise an alarm before the militants succeeded in dragging them inside the basement. A large posse of troops led by a lieutenant colonel reached the spot and asked the militants to release the captives. But the terrorists first wanted to talk to Giani Sahib Singh, one of the head priests. Desperate, the army summoned Sahib Singh, who tried to persuade the militants to release the armymen. But the captors now insisted that the priest come into the basement to talk to them. Obviously, the army smelt a rat. Giani Sahib Singh also panicked and flatly told the army he expected no remorse from those hiding inside. After repeated warnings, the army decided to storm the basement. At the end of a fierce, short engagement, all the militants, and a couple of army jawans lay dead. In the heap of bodies was Captain Rampal, his arms severed, and body mutilated with wounds from bullets as well as sharp-edged weapons. The following day, the commandos and other troops went about scouring the buildings for basements and tunnels. It was in the course of one of these operations that Lieutenant Colonel Chowdhury, Commandant of the SFF commandos battalion, was shot in the shoulder even while President Zail Singh went about examining the damage and saying his prayers in the temple.

From a purely military point of view, an operation of this kind had never been carried out anywhere in the world and the lessons of Bluestar would be analyzed not only in the Indian Army's College of Combat at Mhow but perhaps also at numerous military academies all over the world. It is often said in diplomatic and international military circles now that an operation of this kind could have been carried out much more effectively and with much less bloodshed by a specialized force like the British army's SAS. But Indian commanders point out that even the best commando outfit in the world, whether SAS or American Green Berets, would have found it difficult to break through such fortifications while facing constraints of saving a whole lot of sensitive buildings and installations. Besides, the very intricately political nature of the operation ensured that there was to be no surprise. On the other hand, the army was to make itself highly visible to overawe the defenders and then lie in wait, repeatedly giving warnings. It were these constraints that made a clean, surgical commando operation rather difficult. It ultimately became the much-maligned foot-soldier's battle. Yet, the last-minute twists and turns and the intensity of fighting took the brightest of Indian Army commanders by surprise. Gen Sundarji, formerly director of the College of Combat, latter said that such intense firing had not even been seen during Indo-Pak wars. Dyal, who as a dashing major of the Paras in 1965 had led the remarkable capture of the heavily-held Haji Pir Pass in Pakistan-occupied-

Kashmir, winning a Mahavir Chakra, too had a surprise or two. It was also the most testing experience for Brar, an alumnus of the US army's War College at Carlyle Barracks, Pennsylvania, who too had seen fierce action in 1971, at the head of 1 Maratha in the Bangladesh War, winning a Vir Chakra. All the generals and other officers involved in the operation admit that it was the toughest challenge of their lives, a kind they would not fancy facing again. It is never easy fighting your own countrymen, even more so when they happen to be from a stock which has formed the sword arm of the country's defence for so long.

It is in the light of these complications that the question of an inordinately large number of civilian casualties needs to be examined. One certain contributory factor was the underestimation of the militants' fighting ability. The government and the army brass presumed that with a show of strength by them, the militants would realize the futility of it all and surrender. But as subsequent events showed, this operation was not a Goa or Hyderabad. Also, in such fateful periods, a little bit of luck can make all the difference. And here the army had no luck with the telephones.

It is one of the better guarded secrets of the operation that immediately following the siege, an officer of the Intelligence Bureau and a middle-rank officer of Punjab Police posted in Amritsar had offered to get in touch with Longowal and persuade him to surrender, along with all the pilgrims and unarmed men before the assault. On the eve of the operation, the army had had all the phones disconnected in Amritsar. The telephone authorities were immediately ordered to plug in Longowal's line so that the intelligence men could talk to him. In spite of trying for nearly a day and a half, the telephone men failed to restore the line. Their suspicion was that the cables had somehow been cut. At one stage, the government even offered to cease firing to let the intelligence and policemen go inside to talk to Longowal. The idea was given up as being too risky with no guarantee that the militants would not pick them out. These were, obviously, pre-cellphone days.

So, the battle was joined with nearly a thousand unarmed, innocent men trapped inside the temple complex, forced to witness the concluding stages of one of the most unfortunate chapters in the country's independent history, over half of them ending up dead or wounded. But then, isn't blood, sweat and tears the kind of stuff destinies of nations are built of?

Operation Bluestar: An Eyewitness Account

SUBHASH KIRPEKAR

In Russia, religion is the opium of the people;
In China, opium is the religion of the people.

Edgar Snow

In India, it can safely be said that religion and politics mix like milk and water – and opium is a helpful supplement.

Nowhere is the mix of religion and politics seen so glaringly as in Punjab. This is especially so in the context of the Bhindranwale phenomenon wherein religion was converted into a handmaiden of politics. And not ordinary politics as understood in terms of a democratic framework. But the politics of subversion and secession.

When I met Bhindranwale on the evening of 3 June 1984 in the Akal Takht, I did not know that I was perhaps the last journalist to meet the lion in his den. The meeting took place when the curfew was relaxed between 5 p.m. and 9 p.m.

on 3 June. I entered the Akal Takht at about 6 p.m. and left at 7.30 p.m.

My impression of Bhindranwale was of a man who has somehow usurped the seat of holy authority – a *sant* sans saintliness. His objectives were far from spiritual or religious and I could not see how a division of the country would help the Sikhs. There was something cruel about him, something that disturbed me; but I guess it was this same quality that brought hundreds of youths to him. They were lured by the cult of violence that he succeeded in romanticizing. He impressed upon them that power came out of the barrel of a gun. Maybe it was that mad gleam in his eyes; or the overconfidence with which he conveyed in no uncertain terms that he was the supremo. He looked crafty, like a man who was exploiting his position to influence the gullible.

Bhindranwale had a remarkable way of applying a veneer of Sikhism to all he said. He sought to identify himself with the Sikh community. But from what numerous Sikh friends tell me, they did not identify themselves with him, in any case not at least until the Operation Bluestar was launched.

The shock waves of the military operation have not ceased rippling two months later. There are a large number of Sikhs who appear to be influenced by what some pro-Khalistan Sikhs abroad are saying and doing. But none seems to have recovered enough to question these Sikhs abroad if they would like to come and settle down here or if they are simply interested in fomenting trouble and creating divisions. The unhealthy influence of these elements hostile to India is reflected in the thinking of the Akali Dal and the SGPC. Many find it abhorent to describe Bhindranwale as a martyr and the army as the aggressor. But this is the method that perhaps the Akali Dal and the SGPC have found of shocking the conscience of the nation.

I went to the Golden Temple on the evening of 3 June, somewhat keen on meeting the man everyone dreaded, including those in the Akali Dal and the SGPC.

I walked barefoot down the Parikrama and the causeway to the golden canopied sanctum sanctorum. I knelt before the Guru Granth Sahib, touched my forehead to the ground, prayed and, as on earlier visits, made a small offering. I stretched out my hand for *prasad*. To my surprise, I was asked to proceed (*agey chaliye*). I did not wait to argue; I walked on, looking at the expression of hurt on the faces of those who gazed at the bullet holes on the canopy, the result of the exchange of fire on 1 June.

As I enter the Akal Takht, I am frisked by an armed guard of Bhindranwale at the foot of the narrow, high and winding stairs. Santji is talking to his followers. As I have to wait for some time, I find the conversation with the wiry young Harvinder Singh Sandhu, general secretary of the All India Sikh Students Federation, fairly absorbing. 'All talk of Gandhian *ahimsa* is poppycock,' he remarks. He sees nothing wrong in accepting military assistance from Pakistan because New Delhi sought to treat both, 'Sikhs and Pakistan, as outsiders.'

I am summoned inside. Santji is ready for the interview. We squat face to face on a dirty old floor mat. Behind him sits Amreek Singh, president of the banned AISSF. Here are some excerpts from the interview:

Q: What do you think of the army takeover in Punjab?

A: It is done to suppress the Sikhs. But the government will not succeed. Previous regimes have also never succeeded in such efforts.

Q: Do you believe that the army will enter the Golden Temple?

A: No, the army will hang around this place like the CRP and BSF have done for the last two years. Except truth and justice, nothing but evil is expected of this government. It is premature to say anything about the timing of the entry (of the army) and its possible impact. Their behaviour and intentions will be known in a few days.

Q: **What do you think of Longowal as a leader?**

A: No comments.

Q: **Will you not be outnumbered by the army which has superior weapons too?**

A: Sheep always outnumber the lions. But one lion can take care of a thousand sheep. When the lion sleeps, the birds chirp. When it awakes, the birds fly away. There is silence (laughs).

Q: **Did you listen to the prime minister's speech yesterday?**

A: No, there is no need to; it is not important.

Q: **Do you support the creation of Khalistan?**

A: I never opposed it; nor have I supported it (looks at me rather jubilantly to see if I am impressed by his taciturn reply).

Q: **But is it your contention that the Sikhs cannot live in India?**

A: Yes. They can neither live in nor with India. If treated as equals, it may be possible. But frankly speaking, I don't think that is possible.

Q: **What can be done to stop the slayings of people, including journalists, in Punjab?**

A: (Raising one eyebrow) Ask those who are responsible for it.

Q: **If some harm were to befall you, who would be your successor?**

A: (With a quizzical look in his eyes) Time will tell. I can't name anyone. It is not an elective post. I think whosoever attains the status of God will come up as my successor. (Even as I discern a trace of pomposity in his voice, I also notice a flicker in Amreek Singh's eyes, his first movement since the interview began, as he sat like a marble white statue of a handsome Greek god).

Q: **Do you fear death?**

A: (Eyes nearly blazing with anger) He is not a Sikh who fears death and he who fears death is not a Sikh.

It is now Santji's turn to question me. 'Do you know this man?' he asks, pointing to the elderly Sikh in a silk kurta and a flowing grey-white beard. 'No,' I reply. Santji finds my reply hard to believe. You have never seen him, he asks again, he is Shabeg Singh, a former major general.

Oh yes, of course, Shabeg Singh. The major general who was court-martialled and sacked from the army, suspected of directing the Dashmesh Regiment; and known to be the chief adviser to Bhindranwale in fortifying the Golden Temple complex and procuring the weapons with which to wreak vengeance on the Indian Army. The former major general said he had every right to be beside Santji as an Akali Dal member. If some ex-generals could join the Congress, why could he not join the Akali Dal, he asked.

If we cannot defend the temple, it is not worth being a Sikh, he commented. He had no qualms in describing Santji as God incarnate. The army was here to liquidate Santji, he said, and was confident that death would not affect him in any way.

How soon did he expect the army to start its action? 'Maybe tonight,' he said grimly. The reply jolted Sandhu into reality. Married on 5 May to the daughter of a wealthy Sikh businessman in Bombay, Sandhu must have begun thinking of ways to stay alive.

Shabeg Singh posed for a picture outside in the balcony. Then, he did not want to be disturbed as he began looking from a pair of binoculars at an army position in a tall building opposite.

As I walked out of the Akal Takht, and along the Parikrama to the Ghantaghar, I felt that several pairs of eyes were upon me, watching every step. I expected a burst of fire any minute, so tense was the atmosphere. An eerie silence gripped the whole area. Something terrible was going to happen.

What? And when? I asked myself as I drove back to the Amritsar International Hotel. I settled down to write my story along the lines that 'the army seemed poised for a major crackdown on terrorists and extremists entrenched inside the Golden Temple...'

But it was of no use. The cops were in the hotel. All links with New Delhi were snapped. There was no way of getting the story out. Would I like to be taken to Jullundur? the Inspector asked me. It is a futile night vigil on 3 June. There are no lights in the Golden Temple. But from the hotel terrace, I can see that it is bathed in a glare of floodlights. There is something being said on the loudspeakers. I cannot hear the words, but it might be an appeal to those inside to come out and surrender.

It is at 4.43 a.m. on 4 June that the suspense is broken. The action begins. The deafening boom of guns shatter the stillness, sending flocks of birds screeching in the air. The target appears to be the gun positions atop a tall building near the Akal Takht. I can see sandbags in the brief flash accompanying the red ball of fire striking sand and brick. Light machine-gun fire is returned.

But after that initial firing, there is a lull. There are only sporadic bursts of fire the next day. It seems as if the army is holding back fire after sending out feelers to test the mood and reaction of the militants. The latter replies shot for shot, not wasting any ammunition.

That evening, well before sunset, I hear the unmistakable rumble of tanks. To begin with, it was one tank and one APS (armoured personnel carrier). An hour later, there are a dozen tanks and a dozen APCs in all. The stage is set for the battle of the Golden Temple. In half an hour, eight to ten thundering blasts shook the city of Amritsar. The tanks are positioned at Sultanwind.

After dark, the cops come in again. I am hustled out of the hotel. Clear your bills and take your bags, I am told. They take me to Ritz Hotel. Sheetal Das, SP, is in a temper. Mark Tully of the BBC has told him he will not leave for New Delhi that very night but the next morning. A top brass of the army tells Sheetal Das outside the portico: all foreign correspondents and all Indian correspondents representing foreign papers: OUT.

Only two Indian correspondents stay behind. I am one of them. But I do not wish to stay in Ritz. Though owner Mehra is a charming person, the hotel terrace hardly offers a glimpse of the scene of action. I am permitted to return to my hotel. And my reentry delights the staff which is discussing my fate.

Just when the bus-load of foreign correspondents and Indians working for foreign newspapers is driving out of Amritsar early that morning does the day's action begin. It is 4.45 a.m., 5 June.

The first few shots of 5 June are out of a war film. As a shell crashes on to a rooftop pillbox, the construction material goes up in a cloud of reddish dust. Another boom and I see sandbags and bricks being tossed up high in the air. A cloud of smoke billows up. There is a rapid exchange of fire. Knowing the astronomical rate at which modern weapons spew bullets per second, it is obvious that in the first round of combat, precious lives have been lost on both sides.

The reverberating bursts of fire are followed by death-like silence. Two helicopters circle high above the temple complex thrice. They disappear and radio gun positions that have to be knocked out. Firing starts again. The rat-a-tat of guns is heard all day long.

The mellifluous strains of the *Shabad Gurbani* come wafting with the breeze. There is prayer on one hand, combat on the other. It is an unprecedented combination. I had covered the 1971 liberation of Bangladesh as a war correspondent and seen part of the 1965 Indo-Pak conflict in Khemkaran, Burki and Icchogil Canal. But the environment of battle here and its cause are vastly different. Never before has our army been given the task of flushing out terrorists and extremists from a place of worship.

All of 5 June, the Akal Takht is under fierce attack. The outer line of defence around the temple complex is gradually knocked out. Militants firing from atop the high water tank are silenced. Around high noon a shell hits one of the tanks. And water gushes out like a water fall. The strange sight is visible for almost half an hour. The tank has a capacity of about 10,000 gallons. Then, after it dries up, there is the darkened gaping hole only, a reminder of the action for weeks and months to come.

The Burj or old observation towers built during Ranjit Singh's time are vantage positions for Bhindranwale's men. The 150-year old towers with their almost impregnable thick walls take a lot of banging.

Indeed, the entire attention appears to be focused on one tower from where the militants are letting loose a volley of fire. So heavy is the pall of dust and thick smoke arising from the counterattack that at one stage, it appears that the tower is tilting and is about to fall. But nothing of the kind is happening. My vision is playing tricks on me. It is not built by the CPWD, quips my Sikh friend.

Next to be taken up for demolition is the Langar. Clouds of smoke rise to tell their own story. And from wherever Bhindranwale's men fire, the army fires right back.

June 5, 1.15 p.m. the shelling of the Akal Takht begins. Till 3.35 p.m., there are light exchanges of gunfire interspersed by heavy bouts followed by silence. The air is hot with the energy expended from guns of all sizes and shapes. At 3.45 p.m., half a dozen helicopters fly in formation of threes. They keep away from the temple complex. I wonder who the VIPs are. At 6.20 p.m., there is a shell burst at the overhead tank, indicating that all areas are not yet clear. At 6.40 p.m., there are reddish clouds of smoke arising from the vicinity of the Akal Takht. Fifteen minutes later, two tanks are on the move. At 7 p.m. I see the first corpse carrier vehicle going towards the Chatiwind cremation ghat. The death toll has begun.

The breeze carries an acrid smell, the sickly, clinging smell of burnt flesh.

The night of 5 and 6 June is perhaps the fiercest. The gun fire reaches a deafening crescendo, drowning the *kirtan*. Both sides are giving it all they have. It is as if a last-ditch battle is on. The ferocity with which Bhindranwale's men are fighting demonstrates that they have plenty of weapons and ammunition and that they will not give up, come what may. Though his men in the nine-storeyed golden-domed Baba Atal Gurdwara have been annihilated, though most of the fortifications have been blown to smithereens, they want to fight to the last man, the last bullet. There is no buckling under pressure.

For the first time, I sense that my friends are wondering whether the army has not taken too long to complete the task. A mere Sant has held them at bay for three days. Some of the markets around the temple complex have caught fire. I can see huge flames leaping up and dancing devilishly in the air. I wonder whether the entire city will be engulfed in flames if the fire spreads.

On 6 June I see that the clock towers are structurally intact but the clocks have been broken. The helicopter resumes its aerial surveys. Twice, there is firing at the Baba Atal Gurdwara. One of the bursts leaves a black blob on the white face of the stately gurdwara. There is hardly any abatement of the clouds of smoke that come up all night from the areas in the walled city which have caught fire. This blanket of smoke is pushed by the breeze in the direction of the Pakistan border about 15 kilometres away.

There is a lull in firing at about 8 a.m. but soon thereafter, tank fire blasts shake up Amritsar again. But relatively lighter guns are used to fire at the clock towers from where snipers are shooting away. They are silenced. It seems that during periods of lull, both sides take up fresh positions. Word goes around that the men are out on the Parikrama now and the army is seeking to enter the temple complex. By 10 a.m., there is intense firing. My friends express concern over the impact the military operation will have on communal harmony. It is said that the army is in such an awkward position that neither can it extricate itself now nor go ahead swiftly because of the unexpectedly stiff resistance.

On the afternoon of 6 June, curfew is relaxed for two hours. Since all vehicles are banned everyone is walking. All roads lead to Darbar Sahib. People spill on to the roads like potatoes bursting from a sack. I join the multitude. The SSF boys in their blue battle uniforms are standing near the Dharam Singh Market. Between the Kotwali and the Jallianwala Bagh, there are four tanks. And another three tanks are lined up outside the Ghantaghar. The crowd watching the pockmarked exterior of the temple walls and broken clock forms a 100-deep phalanx. Some of the Sikhs and Hindus fold their hands in prayer from the middle of the road.

As I enter a side lane, I see an army truck emerging. Its cargo is two dead jawans. They are laid on the rear benches as if they are asleep.

On the streets further in, I see corpses of two civilians. People cover their face and nose with a handkerchief.

I wonder why this area was thrown open to the people. Obviously, the army truck driver had no inkling that curfew would be relaxed. Or else he would not have been driving into a huge crowd.

On the way back to the hotel, I witness a scene at the Kotwali which is blood curdling. This is where some jawans were kicking some of the 11 suspected terrorists as they knelt on their bare knees and crawled on the hot road surface. Among the officers directing this operation was a Sikh. His face contorted in anger when he lashed out at his fellowmen who he thought were traitors. But the hundreds of spectators who saw this incident felt anguished. The sight put them off.

A journalist colleague of mine based in Amritsar tells me

that Bhindranwale has moved from the Akal Takht to Harmandir Sahib and has put up LMGs and MMGs all around it and that Tohra and Sant Longowal had surrendered and been moved to a safe place. The first part of his news was incorrect. By that time, Bhindranwale is dead. His body is found on the night of 5-6 June.

There is more firing that night (6 and 7 June). Indeed, I hear the longest burst of fire at 6.30 p.m., barely an hour after curfew is reimposed. There is intermittent fire thereafter. At 5.30 a.m. on 7 June, I see thick black clouds of smoke come out from the vicinity of the Guru Nanak Niwas. If there is a fire there, it does not spread. What is this fire which sends up cloud after cloud of black smoke? And why the putrid smell? Someone on the terrace suggests that corpses are being burnt. This smoke continues for a good two-and-a-half hours.

Akashvani reports that the dead body of Jarnail Singh Bhindranwale has been found. Curfew is to be relaxed at 3 p.m. on 7 June for two hours. A whole lot of people are eagerly waiting at roundabouts and intersections to go into the walled city. But a last-minute announcement cancels the relaxation and orders people to go home. There is a shoot-at-sight order. Everyone scampers homewards. Once again, the streets are deserted.

How may people do you think were killed in Amritsar during Operation Bluestar? I am often asked this question wherever I go. It is not easy to answer. But from the movement of Amritsar municipal garbage vans that ferried the dead, I have a feeling the number of dead is much more than is officially stated. Going by the rumour-mills in Amritsar, the casualty figure is over 2,000. But I have no way to substantiate this as most cremations were done under curfew.

Many people in Amritsar are reported missing. One of these is 26-year-old Raman Inder who worked in the Family Planning Department. He has been missing since 25 June. And the scooter on which he was riding has been found on the outskirts of the city. Where is Raman Inder? The disposal of corpses posed a great problem. So much so that seven truck cleaners behind my hotel were rounded up one morning and threatened with dire consequences if they did not do as ordered. But they stubbornly refused. So the scouts then went to contact some sweepers. They too refused. But when offered liquor and the lure of owning whatever was found on the corpse, be it gold chain or ring or cash, goes the story, they agreed. Some of them have made tidy fortunes in the bargain.

If entering Amritsar on 3 June was a stroke of luck, leaving on 13 June was an achievement. For on 12 June, I had been turned away from the queue because I did not have details like the name of the driver and the taxi number. This time, I was all ready. Even the vehicle and the driver were standing outside if any further confirmation was necessary. The application was approved by the additional district collector and a lieutenant colonel in civvies. The 'travel permit' was issued after several entries in various ledgers, both civil and military.

We were repeatedly stopped and checked for weapons. 'Open the dicky; open the bonnet; open the glove compartment; take out the seats,' barked the jawans with Stenguns at the ready. Mounted light machine-guns were positioned on either side of the road. The Beas Bridge was the most heavily guarded place en route to Chandigarh. There were seven 'hammersledge' tanks on either side of the bridge. And the place was crawling with armed jawans.

I almost got into a jam at Mohali which came under curfew at 8 p.m. We got there about ten minutes later. An aggressive jawan was itching to provoke us. I asked to see his senior. In his presence, I stated that multiple checking had delayed us. Go back from where you came, he told me. I explained that If we did that, we were sure to be shot because our travel permit allowed us to go to Chandigarh. We dare not travel in the reverse direction. We could not disobey army orders. That did it. He told us to proceed to Chandigarh. But move fast, he said.

We will go like the wind, I assured him as Gurdip Singh stepped on the accelerator.

I came to Amritsar again on 17 July. As I flew in I could see the glittering golden canopy of Harmandir Sahib. The surroundings looked serene. But I knew what the complex had undergone almost a month earlier. The city looked different this time. The marks of tank chains on the tar roads had disappeared. Army vehicles moved about. But the jawans were not pointing their weapons outwards any longer as was the case in June.

There was no curfew except for a day and a half when the Nihang chief Baba Santa Singh began his *kar seva* by clearing the Akal Takht debris. Even as many Sikhs resented the Nihang chief undertaking this project of voluntary service and some of them derisively called it *sarkar seva*, it was clear that the move to repair the Akal Takht was fraught with hazards as far as it hurt the Sikh sentiments.

Nevertheless, there are two sides to the case. One is the Akali Dal's which wants the Akal Takht to remain in the present ruinous state as a monument to the army's aggression. The status quo will help the Akali Dal as it does have some hold over the religious and simple village folk. They can be exploited politically with the bogey of their religion being in danger. The other is the government view that repairs must be carried out quickly so that people look to the future instead of brooding over the past. In this approach, hope replaces despair.

How genuine is the *kar seva*? Is it a farce? These questions are posed in many places. The answer is simple: there are two political parties, each sponsoring a Baba. While the Akali Dal advised its Baba octogenarian, Baba Kharak Singh, not to carry out *kar seva* unless the army is withdrawn from the temple complex. Baba Santa Singh points out that after all, it is the Indian Army that is there and not a foreign army. So long as it does not interfere with his work, he has no complaints against it.

When I met Baba Kharak Singh at Chabhal, about 25 kilometres outside Amritsar and close to the Indo-Pak border, he said he would neither criticize nor praise Santa Singh's work. He had moved out of Amritsar because he did now wish to be badgered by various factions, some wanting him to carry out *kar seva* and others pressing him not to.

It is with disdain that the 62-year-old Baba looks upon the order excommunicating him after declaring him a *tankhaiya* (one who commits a Sikh religious offence). 'I am doing constructive work,' he asserts and challenges the right of these paid employees of the SGPC to take any action against him. 'Why was no *hukumnama* issued by the five head priests, when Bhindranwale had turned the temple complex into a fortress?' asks Santa Singh.

I met the five head priests in the Guru Ram Das Hospital. They had returned from their visit to the temple complex where they stood for a few minutes near the Akal Takht. They sat on two hospital beds. They declined to answer questions as they said they wanted to discuss the case of Baba Santa Singh.

Later that evening of 21 July, I visited the residence of Giani Kirpal Singh, *jathedar* of Akal Takht, and spoke to him for an hour and a half. Here are some excerpts from the interview:

Q: Baba Santa Singh asks why no hukumnama was issued when Bhindranwale ensconced himself in the Akal Takht. What is your reply?

A: We did not issue any *hukumnama* because no one complained to me about this matter.

Q: Do you need someone to complain before you can consider any issue?

A: Yes. It has now come to be known that the Indian Institute of International Understanding did make a request to Giani Kirpal Singh to issue a *hukumnama* vide their registered letter of 12 March 1984, copies of which were sent to *jathedars* of all the other takhts and to Mr Longowal, Akali Dal president, and Mr Tohra, SGPC president.

Q: Did anyone complain against Baba Santa Singh undertaking kar seva?

A: Yes.

Q: Who?

A: The Akali Dal and the SGPC.

Q: Did the Dal and SGPC also lodge any complaint when Bhindranwale was ruling the roost in the Akal Takht?

A: No, no one complained. Why did Baba Santa Singh not emerge at that time. Why has he come on the scene now?

Q: Since you are the jathedar of the Akal Takht, the nation was expecting you to do something about it. Were you threatened to keep silent or face the gun?

A: There were several reasons why we could not protest against the happenings inside the Akal Takht and the temple complex. I cannot disclose them now.

Q: Is not the SGPC responsible for the proper management of gurdwaras? Would you say the gurdwaras have been managed properly?

A: I do not wish to make comments.

Q: The Akali Dal and SGPC representatives, Mr Prakash Singh Majitha and Mr Major Singh Uboke, say that Bhindranwale is the 'martyr' and the army the 'aggressor' or hamlawar. Do you agree or disagree with this view?

A: It is for people to decide who can be called *shaheed* and who is the *hamlawar*.

Q: Who according to you can be called shaheed?

A: '*Jo nek kam ke liye marta hai woh shaheed hai*' (he who dies for a good cause is a martyr).

Q: Who died for a good cause: the army officers and jawans who wanted to liberate the Golden Temple and restore sanctity, or Bhindranwale?

A: The army was the *hamlawar.*

Q: Why did you permit Bhindranwale to make the Akal Takht his residence? When I met him inside the Akal Takht on the evening of 3 June, I was searched for weapons by his men and then allowed to go to the second floor. You had no control on the Akal Takht whatsoever as its jathedar?

A: (Very weakly) He did not live in the Akal Takht but in a building behind it.

Q: But how is it that most newsmen had earlier met him in the Akal Takht itself? He had all the rooms to himself there.

A: I do not wish to comment.

Q: Do you think that religion and politics ought to be separated?

A: No. They are inseparable. The government mixes religion with politics. Why should we not do it? Every person is both religious and political. Religion is the soul and politics the body. We Sikhs have religion only. Our dharma is to punish the oppressor. We may be weak politically, but our forte is religion.

Q: When Bhindranwale ordered the killings, could he not be treated as an oppressor and punished?

A: Bhindranwale helped the Congress against the Akali Dal and the SGPC in 1979. The government allowed him to roam freely in New Delhi with weapons. All this was done to give us a bad name and humiliate us. He was a Congress agent.

Q: You are right when you say he should have been arrested. But why did you thereafter allow this Congress agent to gang up with the Akali Dal and the SGPC and dominate the show? You consider him a martyr now.

A: Ask the Akali Dal and SGPC leaders. I don't know.

Q: Don't you think Baba Santa Singh can become another Bhindranwale as some Akali leaders are saying?

A: Don't ask me.

Q: One last question. Some people say Bhindranwale is still alive. What is your information?

A: I was told that he was alive at 9 a.m. on 6 July. I don't know.

Throughout the interview, Giani Kirpal Singh gave the impression of a man who was disillusioned and demoralized. On questions involving Bhindranwale, he would lower his eyes and one discerned a trace of fear. It was as if there was some *bandookwala* hiding behind the curtain and almost as if he was afraid of losing something precious if he became more forthright. I had hoped that Giani would be talking freely and fearlessly now that Bhindranwale was no more. But he looked a haunted man, weak-willed, confused and brainwashed.

A word about the terrorists abroad. I am told by Mr V. Ram, principal of the International Gandhi Memorial School in Jakarta, that five youths belonging to the banned AISSF landed up in Jakarta on 8 July. They established contact with him through some students. They told him that if they did not secure their no-objection certificates from the Indian Embassy there to proceed to USA and Australia, they would do something drastic. They could have blown up the Indian Embassy building which was inaugurated on 4 June by the then Foreign Minister, Mr P.V. Narasimha Rao. Or they could have played hell in the Sikh gurdwara in Pasabari where they were about to take shelter.

Mr Ram, who is popularly regarded in Jakarta as India's 'unofficial ambassador' and is a staunch nationalist, pacified the youths. He told them that the situation in Jakarta was such that if they resorted to any violence, the Indian community would not appreciate it at all. And they would be severely dealt with by the Indonesian police and army. On his persuasion, they did not stay in the gurdwara.

The Indian ambassador in Indonesia, Gen O.P. Malhotra, was informed about the AISSF youths by his military attache and first secretary. The youths confessed that they were suspected of having assassinated Ramesh Chander, editor of *Hind Samachar* group of newspapers in Jullundur. He was killed on 12 May 1984 and since then these youths had been on the run.

In Amritsar and New Delhi, the hot debate is on issues that boil down to perspectives. In one scenario, the army is the villain. It has desecrated the Golden Temple and anguished Sikh feeling by the excessive force used in Operation Bluestar. In the other scenario, Bhindranwale is the villain, and the army is the liberator. It is Bhindranwale who desecrated the temple complex by converting the Akal Takht into an arsenal and a place to stock the loot from robbed banks. There was a harem of village girls for the pleasure of his brainwashed brigade. Some of these girls are said to be pregnant now. In this scenario, had not Bhindranwale ensconced himself in the Akal Takht, it would never have been attacked.

There are some who talk of blood and tears in a pool of nectar. They would be applying the healing touch if they also spoke of the dangers of marigold and roses being replaced by deadly weapons in a sacred shrine.

The Akali Dal, the SGPC and the five head priests talk repeatedly of Bhindranwale being a creation of the Congress. But I find that they are hard put to explain why they are out to make the Congress discard their martyr. The hypocrisy and double-facedness stands exposed.

When they lay emphasis on the Akal Takht as an institution, and not as a mere building, being damaged they fail to see why the army doctor Capt Shyam Sunder Rampal should have had his hands chopped off by terrorists and bled to death; or why Dr V.N. Tiwari, MP, should have been gunned down in his Chandigarh residence; or why Ramesh Chander was slain in Jullundur. If *hukumnamas* of the past few hundred years have been destroyed, none can rejoice over this tragedy. But can Bhindranwale be absolved of the blame for this sorry situation?

Some stalwarts talk about different solutions that might have been possible to implement. Prominent among these theories is that the army could have laid a siege to the Golden Temple and given an ultimatum. Water, power, food supplies, etc., could have been cut off during the siege to force the entrenched men out. This, however, would not have worked. For one thing, the Golden Temple complex does have a few tunnels leading into houses in different areas. This would have enabled a determined Bhindranwale to make a monkey out of the army to appear at a venue and time of his choice. Secondly, the gullible villagers could have been made to believe that Sikhism was in danger and asked to encircle the army. Such a situation would have led to greater bitterness and more bloodshed without achieving results. The last two-and-a-half years of Bhindranwale's reign of terror cannot be wiped out from the collective memory of the people in the north; nor can it be shrugged off as an ugly nightmare.

To ensure that such a reign of terror is not unleashed again, it is necessary that my Sikh friends who talk of alienation stop identifying themselves with Bhindranwale. If most Sikhs rightly did not support him during his lifetime, why should they now bestow this posthumous popularity on him?

If the Congress made the mistake of creating Bhindranwale, then the Akali Dal, SGPC and the five head priests are committing a blunder by trying to make a martyr out of what ostensibly was a monster. What is the rationale behind the argument that Bhindranwale with the Congress is evil but with the Akali Dal is a saint?

Let it be recalled that when Sir Aroor Singh, the manager of the Golden Temple in 1919, presented a *saropa* to General Dyer immediately after the massacre in next door Jallianwala Bagh, the Sikhs raised a furore. They felt that great injustice had been done to all.

There is sufficient evidence to believe that Bhindranwale entertained anti-national and secessionist ambitions. If his objectives were within the democratic framework, why did he need to pile up arms and ammunition? It is pointless to accuse the authorities of planting weapons inside the temple complex. Once it is realized that the military action was not against the Sikhs as a community, but against the extremist leader Bhindranwale, it should not be difficult to remove the trauma which is distorting the thinking of the Sikhs. Hence the need to look at events in their entire perspective.

Assault on the Golden Temple Complex 5-6 June 1984

LT GEN JAGJIT SINGH AURORA (RETD)

Since Independence, it was for the first time that the Indian Army had been employed to fight a pitched battle against a section of its own people. The assault on the Golden Temple on 5-6 June 1984 turned a shrine of great sanctity into a battlefield. This has shocked and angered the Sikh masses and caused anguish to many more of other religious beliefs. The immediate question that arises is: was the army action really necessary? Was it the only solution? My view is that it was not.

To begin with, the Akali agitation had lasted for so long that it was obvious to anyone that it would continue till certain political demands were met. These demands were of all Punjabis; only, the Akali party had taken the initiative to agitate for them. Unfortunately the political demands were mixed up with some religious demands and the Akalis failed to carry Punjabi Hindus with them and later even alienated them. The only way to end the agitation was to find an answer to these political demands. The longer the solution was delayed, the more complicated the problem became. Had the government been sincere to find an answer it could have done so far more easily in the earlier stages.

Whenever the Akalis found their agitation flagging or losing momentum they came out with a new demand to keep it going. The delay also acted in favour of Jarnail Singh Bhindranwale whose violent methods further alienated the Hindus. The government clearly failed to foresee the direction in which the situation was developing and by not acting in time caused great grief to the Sikhs and much harm to the national integrity.

The second important reason is that if a correct assessment had been made of Bhindranwale's role and his religious fanaticism, and if it was realized that no compromise with him was possible, action against him should have been taken much earlier. One must not forget that Bhindranwale had been taken into custody by the then chief minister, Darbara Singh, but was released under mysterious circumstances. Worse still, he (Bhindranwale) was allowed to travel all over India with an armed bodyguard like a conquering hero. This established his image in Punjab as a man with whom the government was reluctant to tangle. It added to his charisma as a religious and popular leader.

If one is to believe Harkishan Singh Surjeet, and I see no reason to disbelieve him, he had claimed, both from public platforms and in writing, that many discussions were held between the Akali party and the central government when differences were narrowed down considerably and decisions were practically arrived at, but at the last minute talks were broken off by the government. As a result the moderate Akali leadership, eager to end the crisis, was forced to return to Amritsar empty-handed each time, where it was jeered at by the Bhindranwale group who said, 'Well, if you go with a begging bowl what do you expect? Unless you can stand up to this government you'll get nothing.' Slowly and steadily, the Akalis found themselves losing credibility among the Sikh masses, and

Bhindranwale's influences increasing. My conviction is that if Sant Harchand Singh Longowal's position had not been weakened by these unfruitful negotiations, he and the others would have been able to control Bhindranwale. All the same it is a pity that the head of the SGPC, Gurcharan Singh Tohra, permitted Bhindranwale to shift from Guru Nanak Niwas to Akal Takht and entrench himself there.

Another glaring anomaly in the government's decision was to cloak the Operation Bluestar in such secrecy. In my opinion when an action is to be taken against a section of your own people, as against a foreign enemy, it is wiser to take the nation into confidence rather than be secretive. Before embarking on such an unprecedented operation it should have been realized that whatever the circumstances, the Sikhs would be hurt badly if the Golden Temple complex was assaulted. It was essential, therefore, to try and create a favourable public opinion amongst the Sikhs by informing them that the situation had deteriorated to such an extent that no other course was possible. To convince them a conclave of Sikh saints and prominent Sikhs could have been called and they could have been asked to persuade Sant Jarnail Singh Bhindranwale to vacate the temple complex. Even the *Jathedars* of the five Takhts could have been invited to this conclave and asked to issue a *Hukumnama* against storing of arms in the Golden Temple. Only if these efforts had failed then and only then should the final step have been taken. There is every likelihood that Bhindranwale would have found it difficult to go against the *Hukumnama* and the whole tragedy would have then been avoided. To counter this argument it may be suggested that there would have been adverse reactions from the villages where Sant Bhindranwale was extremely popular and even venerated. Groups of armed villagers would have started marching towards Amritsar and it would have become very difficult to control them. This happened in any case when rumours of impending army action and the damage to the Golden Temple complex by the army spread. The army, however, was able to prevent these crowds from entering Amritsar city mostly by show of force. Only on few occasions fire had to be opened. The fear of mass Sikh peasantry entering the town of Amritsar to burn and pillage it, was entirely unfounded. It is beyond one's comprehension why a popularly elected government tried to act surreptitiously in an hour of national crisis. If the government believes that the majority of the Sikhs are nationalists why did it not give them a chance to prove themselves? It will take a long time before this anguish and sense of alienation begins to fade and the Sikhs once again feel that they are a part of the Indian nation.

One of the strongest features of the Sikh community before this action was that despite being a minority, very few actually felt that they did not belong to the national mainstream, as they have lived harmoniously with all other communities; the fact that they looked different or had a different religion was never a consideration for them to feel apart. Now they do. And this is highly unfortunate both for the Sikhs and for the integrity of the country.

I went to Amritsar on 6 July, visited the Golden Temple and talked to the army authorities and others who were there during the army operation. The damage to the entire complex was much beyond what was reported in the media news or the press. It was difficult not to feel hurt and to control one's anguish. It is not easy to rationalize when your deepest sentiments are injured.

I consider that the Operation was put through in a great rush. Detailed reconnaisance and deliberate planning was not done. The army has blamed the intelligence authorities for lack of information but what stopped the army from confirming, rejecting or supplementing the information given by personal reconnaisance by the concerned commanders and other key personnel? These reconnaisances could have or should have been done before the main forces came on the scene. June 5 was not a sacrosanct date. In fact it was a bad choice. That year 3

June was Guru Arjan Dev's martyrdom day. On that day a large number of Sikh devotees visited the Golden Temple. That was the day when curfew was imposed in the entire city. When the city administration realized that it was the fifth guru's martyrdom day they first lifted the curfew for sometime and then reimposed it. It is now believed by people that many of the devotees were not able to come out and later were killed during the military action. This could have been avoided if the Operation was undertaken a few days later. With all the time at their disposal, when the government decided to go ahead with this Operation they did so in a great hurry, which resulted in many more deaths and much more damage to the complex. Had more time been permitted for planning and preparation, a way could have been found to deal with the extremists occupying the Akal Takht from the back through the built-up area. As it was, some of the high buildings around the complex had been occupied by the CRPF and BSF before the army arrived. More could have been occupied by them to give army personnel suitable jumping-off places to surround the Akal Takht from the rear. But, the army did not seem to have enough time to consider these possibilities.

The plan which was executed seems to have underrated the resistance the army was likely to meet or was so much influenced by the other considerations that it suffered from adhocism. I do not wish to question the army's competence or the commanders' ability. I have always felt and still feel that under the circumstances and the compulsions imposed on them they completed a difficult assignment successfully and with great care. The fault mainly lies in not permitting them enough time which was required for proper planning and preparation. I did raise the question of outflanking the Akal Takht. I was told that the area was so heavily built up, that it was not feasible to infiltrate through such an area. I maintain that an attack by infiltration from behind the Akal Takht together with the frontal attack should have been attempted in order to get the defenders facing two or three directions. As it happened the troops had to go through the Parikrama and came under prearranged fire wherever they went. It appeared that the army simply did not have the time to consider these possibilities before they actually ringed the temple complex. Once they did so, it became difficult to hide the onset of the action. The troops could have come in only after a preliminary survey had been made by small parties moving about as devotees. Launching the Operation in such a tremendous hurry was, of course, a political decision. It was a mistake that should have been avoided to reduce bloodshed.

Given the constraints of time and other restrictions, one cannot fault the army for using direct approaches and depending on superior firepower as against tactical manoeuvre. They realized that the Operation consisted of two distinct parts: one, of getting Bhindranwale and his men out of Akal Takht and two, bringing Longowal, Tohra and their men safely out of Guru Ramdas Serai. The latter operation was simpler. The troops did meet with some resistance possibly from the armed members of the Babbar Khalsa. They were able to overcome this by the use of superior fire power and took the two leaders into custody together with two or three hundred others who were all unarmed. The White Paper has claimed that Bhindranwale's men succeeded in killing several of these people. I doubt it. There is always some confusion in a battle. These people after being taken into custody were collected in the courtyard of Teja Singh Samundari Hall. Either a grenade thrown by someone or a shell fired by the army landed amongst this group which caused casualties. The army understandably reacted violently and spread into Teja Singh Samundari building where they entered each room after first spraying it with bullets. This resulted in further casualties. It is unlikely that Bhindranwale was planning internecine murders at this stage while he was fighting for his life in the Akal Takht complex.

The securing of the main Golden Temple complex was the crucial task. To overcome the resistance here three to four infantry battalions and two commando groups were employed. They had to be supported by mortar, artillery and tank fire. Although the entry of troops took place from various directions, eventually they all had to traverse over the Parikrama around the Golden Temple and the Sarovar. While approaching the prepared defences over this area troops had to assault over open ground bereft of all cover. This is where they suffered most of the casualties. The commando groups who led the first assault suffered the most. Once inside the quadrangle there was little or no room for manoeuvre. The Akal Takht lies well back and dominates all frontal approaches. It was not easy to close in with the defences located there and the troops had to use tank fire liberally to destroy most of the defences before they could overcome the resistance. The attack started after dark on 5 June. All other areas were cleared of the defenders by the morning of 6 June, but the Akal Takht defences were overcome only by 1 o'clock on the night of 6-7 June. From all accounts the fighting was bitter and no quarters were given or asked.

It is also clear that the army did not expect such resistance from all sides. To save lives first an armoured personnel carrier was used which was disabled as it came close to the Akal Takht defences. Later tank lights were used to blind the defenders to help the infantry close in. This move also failed. Eventually the tanks were brought into the Parikrama and were used to destroy the prepared defences of Akal Takht.

The casuality figures as given out by the authorities are 84 killed and 230(?) wounded on the army side and 493 killed and 86 wounded on the other side. The ratio of killed to wounded is very high as far the army is concerned whereas the ratio from the extremist side would indicate that either they fought to the bitter end or no mercy was shown.

Though the main operation ended with the fall of the Akal Takht defences, mopping up operations continued for the next three days. Suicide squads of Bhindranwale's followers had to be cleared out from the neighbouring buildings. During these operations much damage was caused to private property and many innocent people lost their lives. Unfortunately, dead bodies by the hundreds lay in the open inside the complex which were finally cleared after three days with the help of municipal committee vans. All those killed in the complex were cremated en masse. Relations were not permitted to claim the dead bodies. No proper record of those killed has been drawn up and made available to the public so far. This has led to many rumours, where the numbers of killed have been greatly exaggerated.

It was claimed that the Golden Temple was not damaged during the operations because strict instructions had been issued to the army not to fire in that direction whatever the provocation. In actual fact the Golden Temple had more than 250 bullet marks which I saw with my own eyes. I also saw that there were no prepared defences inside the Golden Temple. There were defences in other parts of the complex – brick-and-mortar and sandbag breast works and bunkers – but none inside the temple. If there was fire from the Golden Temple it would have been certain mobile light machine-gun teams who must have gone there temporarily. Chances are that in the heat of the battle some small arm fire was directed on Harmandir Sahib in spite of the instructions to the contrary. It is understandable. What is not understandable, however, is why the information about the damage was kept a secret. Such secrecy only resulted in the loss of credibility of the government-controlled media.

Besides the destruction of Akal Takht, the loss of the historic library is even more poignant. The building either caught fire or was set on fire and its contents entirely destroyed. Steel shelves containing valuable manuscripts and books lie twisted out of shape in the backyard. The building is being fast repaired but all the ancient handwritten texts and granths, some of them inscribed in the gurus' own hands, have been irretrievably lost. The whole library, in fact, is a burnt out shell. The controversy surrounding the destruction of the library is unfortunate. While the army claims that it caught fire on the morning of 6 June when fighting was in progress, the temple *sevadars* and *granthis* present during the Operation maintain that it was set on fire on 7 June.

It was the use of tanks which eventually enabled the army to overcome the resistance. Without the use of tanks it would have been very difficult and expensive in human lives to capture the Akal Takht. The sequence of events in this Operation shows that plans had to be modified as the situation developed. Maybe the army tried its best to restrain the use of heavier weapons till it was forced to do so. On the other hand it was possibly due to lack of information and incorrect appreciation that the army had to react to unexpected situations. The government's insistence on speed and secrecy – very good weapons in fighting an enemy – caused more damage and confusion when dealing with a section of its own citizens.

Much has been said about the quantum of weapons and preparation of defences by the extremists. When I visited the Golden Temple with my wife in December 1983 and spent two hours one evening and two the following morning, I could see no defences of any description. As a devotee I visited various parts of the temple as well as Baba Atal Gurdwara. There were no signs of any defensive preparation anywhere. Bhindranwale was living in Guru Nanak Niwas at the time. I next visited the Golden Temple on 24 February 1984, by which time he had moved into the Akal Takht building. I saw people carrying weapons in the Parikrama area but there were no fortifications. The top of the Langar building had been fortified with sandbags and I was told there were periodic firings from the CRPF and hence the sandbags had been put up for protection. The defences did not appear very formidable, as anything on top of a building can be knocked off quite easily.

When I visited the temple again on 6 July, exactly a month after the Operation, I saw some of the defences which might have been built over, but a large number had been left to show to the people how the defences had been built by the terrorists. It was obvious that in a period of three months – between March and June – much had been done and the defences had been well sited. I knew Maj Gen Shabeg Singh, who had served under me during the Bangladesh Operation in 1971. He had not lost his professional touch. From the account of the battle as narrated bv Maj Gen K.S. Brar the extremists had taken every advantage of their defensive positions and fought valiantly and skilfully.

So far it has not been possible to assess the strength of the extremists in the Golden Temple complex. It is possible that quite a few of the Babbar Khalsa who were deployed towards Nanak Niwas would have esscaped. In the main complex quite a number of the devotees got trapped because of the curfew on 3 June 1984. Everybody inside the temple was not an extremist or terrorist. From the figures that the army has released – 493 terrorists killed, 86 wounded and more than 1500 taken prisoner – it is clear that many of them were devotees or those who had come to join the peaceful *shahidi jathas* The number of weapons seized, though large, would indicate that these were insufficient to equip a force of more than 2,000 people. The number of weapons seized from all parts of the temple complex, including the Sarovar, were about 1000, which included over a 100 pistols. This only reinforces the argument that a large number of devotees got trapped. It has been mentioned that the terrorists refused to let them out. This is unlikely. It appears that while the army was broadcasting a message asking the people to come out, *shabad kirtan* was in progress and not many heard the army appeal. Also from 4 June onwards continuous firing was going on which forced people to stay indoors. This was confirmed by some of the people who were with Sant Longowal at that time. They only came to know about the appeal at about 5.30 p.m. on 5 June through a messenger. Sant Longowal deputed somebody to check the information but before anyone could get out heavy firing restarted and people went back indoors.

The use and stocking of firearms inside the Golden Temple is reprehensible and inexcusable. I make no excuse for Bhindranwale and his followers for preaching and practising violence as this is against the tenets of Sikhism. There is, however, a need to correct the picture that has been painted by the media that sophisticated weapons were found inside the temple. The first thing to remember is that in a war weapons get lost! In both the wars with Pakistan in 1965 and 1971, a large number of weapons were picked up by people and never accounted for. With the large-scale smuggling going on across Punjab-Pakistan border some gunrunning must have taken place. Since 1960, the government has been issuing arms to certain reliable people living close to the border for security purposes. So there have been a lot of unaccounted weapons in circulation in Punjab, used often in family feuds, property disputes and dacoity. Their buying and selling has been a lucrative trade. Another point to note is that of the weapons seized inside the temple, only 60 self-loading rifles bear foreign markings. The rest are all of Indian origin. Further, there were no medium machine-guns or mortars. There were, however, a large number of light machine-guns. Ammunition for both the light and medium machine-guns is the same, but a medium machine-gun has a higher and more sustained rate of fire. There were two rocket launchers with the terrorists but only one was used. It is obvious, therefore, that there were not so many sophisticated weapons. Quite a lot, yes; but the impression that has been built up in the public mind of foreign governments deliberately arming the terrorists with a view to overthrowing the government is grossly overdone.

I am certain that for the army it has been an extremely unpleasant task. Some of the officers have come under a great deal of criticism. I know both Lt Gen R.S. Dayal MVC and Maj Gen K.S. Brar VrC well. Both had served under me. Dayal was the hero of Hajipeer Pass in 1965 War with Pakistan, while Brar commanded his batallion with distinction in Bangladesh Operations. Both are gallant and capable officers. It is unfair to criticize them for the conduct of this Operation which could not have been of their own choosing. They, however, did not falter and carried out their assignments loyally and to the best of their ability. The actual conduct of the Operation was the responsibility of Brar, but I doubt if he had much freedom in its planning and execution. One thing that impressed me was that before going into the battle he told his troops that if any one did not wish to take part in this Operation he could opt out. This was a fine gesture, though at that time no soldier was likely to back out. In spite of carrying out the Operation successfully, he has had no sense of achievement. He had to spend much of his time explaining why so much damage took place and so many casualties occurred. It is wrong to blame the officers for the shortcomings of higher policy decisions.

At this stage it may be appropriate to evaluate the role of Maj Gen Shabeg Singh whose name has shot up to great prominence after this Operation. I knew him well and first met him in 1948 during the Jammu and Kashmir Operations against Pakistan. For sometime he was a parachutist and so was I. I came in contact with him again in 1963-64 when he was a staff officer in intelligence branch of a Corps Headquarters and I was a divisional commander. During the Bangladesh Operations in 1971, he served under me, when he was employed for training guerillas of the Mukti Bahini. He was competent, enthusiastic and well liked. He was not particularly religious at that time as he used to clip his beard and cut his hair. Shabeg really seemed to enjoy the kind of job he was doing; he got along very well with the Bangladeshi trainees and enjoyed their confidence. He had the capacity to enthuse people around him. I last met him after my retirement when he was area commander in Jabalpur as a major general. Later he was transferred to Bareilly from where he was dismissed for certain administrative irregularities. I had no opportunity or cause to doubt his financial integrity when he was serving under me. In Shabeg Singh I found a useful and valuable officer who enjoyed any job given to him to which he brought much zest and enthusiasm. I recommended him for an Ativashisht Seva Medal which he was given for the Bangladesh Operations. I think he went overboard and joined Bhindranwale together with a number of other army officers who, after leaving the army returned to Punjab, to find how values had changed. Their dissatisfaction stemmed from the fact that the retired servicemen were accorded little respect or consideration by the civil administration. To add fuel to the fire during the Asiad in 1982 when all Sikhs travelling to Delhi from Punjab were stopped and searched regardless of their status or convictions they felt grieved and some of them came under Sant Bhindranwale's influence. In Shabeg's case, his dismissal from service and later harassment by the CBI became a motivating factor. Maybe he got some professional satisfaction, to organize the defences for Sant Bhindranwale's fight against the government. There were other officers who had become Bhindranwale's disciples but did not stick by him till the end. The fact that Shabeg did, and was ready to die for him, speaks as much for his loyalty or bitterness against the government as for Bhindranwale's charismatic appeal.

It is for the first time that desertions on such a scale have taken place from the army. The episode in Ramgarh could be termed a mutiny when the regimental commandant was shot dead by the soldiers. From what one has been able to glean from newspaper reports, one can only surmise that these incidents occurred spontaneously and were not a premeditated plan or deep-seated conspiracy as averred by some. This is apparent from the fact that most of the deserters picked up weapons from their units, got into military transport and left from places like Pune and Ramgarh, hoping to reach Amritsar in large groups!

Even a little bit of clear thinking would have made it obvious to them that they stood no chance of reaching Amritsar without being intercepted, killed or rounded up en route. This is actually what happened. That such an occurrence took place is enough of an indication of the magnitude of emotional reaction they must have felt losing complete balance. More disturbing is the fact that such an event should have taken place in the Indian Army with its unsullied record of discipline and loyalty. Without making excuses for those who deserted or mutinied one cannot help feeling that the authorities failed to foresee that an assault on the Golden Temple complex may lead to such an eventuality. Had the authorities appreciated that fact and taken senior army officers into confidence before hand, they would have had time to prepare their men by explaining to them why the army action was imperative.

Clearing of the terrorists from the Golden Temple complex and other gurdwaras was only Phase I of the Operation Bluestar. As soon as Phase I was over Phase II was launched which was to capture and clear off the terrorists from Punjab countryside. This Operation is still in progress and three or four infantry divisions have been employed on it. To begin with the *modus operandi* was to have the troops located down to *thanas.* Their job was to carry out searches of suspected houses or villages to locate extremists/terrorists. The suspects were taken to interrogation centres and persuaded to confess. Those who were considered innocent were sent back to their villages. Others were handed over to the police custody. Unfortunately; the only method of persuasion appears to be physical coercion. This has led to many hair-raising stories.

It is believed that the army units have now been drawn back to *tehsil* headquarters and most of the searches are being conducted by the police or paramilitary forces. Army units still carry out frequent patrolling of the disturbed or suspected areas.

This prolonged stay of the army on internal security duties has made it rather unpopular amongst the Sikh population.

There are frequent complaints of high-handedness and excesses. There is no doubt that the army action against the Golden Temple and other gurdwaras in Punjab, and its subsequent employment in the rural areas for apprehending the terrorists has caused almost complete polarization between the two communities. The death of Sant Bhindranwale came as a relief to the Hindus but the destruction of Akal Takht was a shock to the Sikhs. Whereas the Sikhs, specially in the villages, want the army to be withdrawn immediately the Hindus are apprehensive that violence against them would start again once the army leaves. There appears to be no meeting ground on this issue. Continued stay of the army in the state cannot solve it. Eventually the two communities have to realize that they have to learn to understand and appreciate each others' fears and suceptibilities. They must let bygones be bygones. This is where the healing touch is required. Who should take the initiative?

Unfortunately the sectarian leadership and the press has been apportioning the blame, rather than promoting unity. The government's attitude and actions have worsened the situation. The official media continues to claim what a wonderful job has been done; that the Golden Temple has been saved which would otherwise have been destroyed; that minimum possible damage was inflicted and the sacred temple, which had been desecrated by the extremists was cleaned up. It is now necessary to ensure that the extremists do not come back to the temple and for this continued employment of the army for its protection is necessary. Neither the SGPC nor the Sikh community as a whole can be trusted to ensure that such a situation will not recur. Without any regard for the Sikh sentiments *kar seva* of Akal Takht has been entrusted to Baba Santa Singh of Budha Dal who hardly represents the Sikh community. All kinds of steps are being taken to boost his image and gather people from various places and groups to show how popular the *kar seva* is. In the meantime devotees are permitted to visit the Golden Temple from 4 to 6 in the morning only. If the *kar seva*, as being carried out now, is acceptable to the majority of the Sikhs where is the need to take such strict measures to ensure that devotees and the people doing *kar seva* are kept segregated? After having declared that on no account fire arms would be permitted inside a place of worship it is surprising to see that the followers of Baba Santa Singh toting rifles while doing *kar seva.* This is certainly not the way to apply the healing touch and assuage the injured feelings of the Sikhs. On one side it is repeatedly claimed that the action was not against the Sikh community but a few extremists who had taken to violence; on the other hand majority of the Sikhs are being hindered from doing *kar seva* to rebuild the Akal Takht with their own hands as labour of love and devotion. It may be mentioned that during the Mughal times when Jahangir offered money for the building of Takht Sahib, Guru Hargobind declined the offer, saying that building of this Takht was the privilege of the community as their personal contribution to the faith. The present method of doing *kar seva* is one sure way of creating differences within the Sikh community which will further destabilize the already unstable situation in the state.

It is a part of the role of the army to help the civilian administration in maintaining law and order if the situation gets out of hand. It is not the sort of role that either the army or the other armed forces would like to undertake. Taking punitive action against your own people is not a pleasant task; but when the need arises it has to be done. However, care should be taken to ensure that the army is not kept deployed on internal security duties for a minute longer than is necessary. Armed forces should command the respect and affection of the civil population. This is a valuable asset during war when the country is facing foreign aggression. If the army is involved in taking punitive measures against its own people for a long time this respect and affection can turn into hatred and belligerence. The use of the army during this episode in Punjab has been extensive and all-embracing. Police had become ineffective and the administration was told not to interfere. The army was given total freedom of action to carry out arrests and investigation. It was permitted to establish its own interrogation centres. People were picked up and kept in custody without giving reasons. By and large the army has acted humanely and with due care. There have been, however, certain incidents where excesses have occurred either due to ignorance or due to over-zealousness on the part of junior leaders. This unfortunately has led to many inflated rumours which have sullied the army's reputation.

In this particular case there is a further danger that it may cause dissensions within the army itself as the majority of the troops employed in this task have been non-Sikhs and the action has been taken against the families or relatives of Sikh soldiers while they are away on duty.

Today, corruption has become a way of life in civil administration but the armed forces are comparatively free of it due primarily to a lack of opportunity and of course discipline. Continued exposure to the civilian method of working and behaviour can have adverse effect on the state of discipline and morale. The Armed Forces of India have so far remained totally apolitical and a model of national and emotional integration and free of communal disharmony. They are the steel frame holding the country together. Their solidarity must not be jeopardized on any account.

It may be worthwhile to consider why the situation in Punjab deteriorated to such an extent that respect for the authority disappeared and a group of extremists were permitted to hold the government, administration, people of Punjab, and even the leaders of Akali party, to ransom. It would be naive to believe that Sant Bhindranwale's fundamentalism was responsible for it. In fact the rise of Sant Bhindranwale and his fantastic hold over the Sikh masses in the rural areas is a phenomenon which needs investigation. There is little doubt that for the last ten years or so the civilian administration everywhere in India has become increasingly ineffective. People are losing faith in getting justice by legal means. Political influence, money power and muscle power are necessary to succeed. Moral deterioration in public life has discouraged people of quality from taking active interest in the country's politics. Party interests and even individual interests take precedence over national interests. The battle of the ballot has become the most important factor while taking decisions on social, political and economic matters affecting the future of the country. No doubt, therefore, that justified grievances of common people are not redressed for a long time. This state of affairs breeds violence. People, especially the hot-headed young ones, lose patience and try to resolve problems by force. This is wrong and reprehensible but to eradicate this tendency repressive measures alone are not enough. The root of the dissatisfaction has to be found and eradicated. Symptomatic treatment at best provides a temporary relief. At the time of election all norms of decency and fairplay are forgotten. Passions are aroused on communal, social, sectarian, caste, creed or any other ground to defeat the rival and get elected. Capturing of booths by strong-arm methods, using money to buy votes misusing authority and preventing people by physical force or violence from casting votes is all acceptable. After the battle of ballot is won how is it possible for people to start obeying and respecting the law of the land and become good citizens? Disrespect for the law of the land has become an all-India issue. The politicians are the biggest defaulters. They are in league with money-bags and criminals who want to hold the country in thrall. Lust for power for self-aggrandizement is the only aim. The youth of the country has, therefore, scant respect either for the elders or for the law of the land. Such a state of affairs is fertile ground for mountebanks, charlatans and fanatics to lead astray the dissatisfied youth.

Democracy grants every individual the right to express his views without fear and favour. If his views differ from those of the party in power the individual does not become unpatriotic or anti-national. In fact an opposition party is considered necessary for a stable democratic country. Why is it that whenever the opposition parties disagree with the party in power today they are dubbed as anti-national? Similarly if a minority community demands a greater voice in its own affairs it becomes suspect. There cannot be two standards, one for the dominant party and the other for the minorities, similarly one for the party in power and the other for the opposition. In spite of whatever has happened and is happening the vast majority of the Sikhs do not want Khalistan and are not asking for it. The pronouncements from the government media as well as much of the national press keeps on stressing that the timely action by the army has just been able to defeat the machinations of the Khalistanis.

Though the army action in the Golden Temple was completed within a week or so, the army is still in occupation. Nearly two months have elapsed and phase II of the Operation Bluestar is still in progress. Special ordinances have been passed to deal with the extremists and terrorists. A large number of people have been taken into custody. No one knows what their fate will be. More arrests take place every day and terrorists' acts still occur. Fear grips the entire state. Periodic pronouncements take place about foreign powers trying to destabilize the country. No foreign power can destabilize a well-knit, contented and cohesive society. They can only fish in troubled waters. Admittedly, India is a complex society and poverty and burdgeoning population has made it impossible to give everyone a satisfying portion of the cake. This should not, however, normally turn people against their own chosen country. One can imagine disgruntled people becoming antisocial but very few will become antinational.

The fact is that in spite of all the bloodshed that has taken place and damage caused, both physical and emotional, the solution to the political problems of Punjab is no nearer than it was before 5 June 1984. In fact it is a bit further away. The

Akalis cannot accept less than their original demands and the government is unwilling to give now what it was willing to give before. In the meantime, purely repressive measures are increasing the divide between the Sikhs and the Hindus not only in Punjab but also in the neighbouring states. The atmosphere in Punjab is ripe to promote extremism and terror but a big stick has never been able to eradicate any insurgency which has popular support.

The ultimate solution lies in compromise and giving the minority community a sense of belonging and trust. It must be accepted that the entire Sikh community is hurt and grieved. But the healing touch applied so far has only increased their anguish. Had the *kar seva* been entrusted to Baba Kharak Singh, the process of healing would have made a start. Now it has become the biggest irritant. An average Sikh feels that he is looked at with suspicion by law-maintaining authorities and is quite often treated rudely. He wonders if he has the same rights and privileges as other nationals of this country. The intellectuals are singled out for having failed to rise to the occasion. When were intellectuals ever consulted or asked to give their advice or views about solving the problem before 5-6 June 1984? Even today all efforts of the public-minded people are put to nought because they go against the political interest of the ruling party.

The situation today is no less fraught with danger than before. In fact it is far more delicate and fragile and requires consumate skill in handling. The government of the day owes it to the people to take definite steps to create a favourable atmosphere where, to begin with, every Sikh does not feel like a culprit. The government should accept the Punjabi political and economic demands unilaterally which will contribute greatly to normalize the situation.

What has been and is happening in Punjab is not the concern of the Punjabis only. It concerns the entire nation. Had a solution been found in time, and it was feasible to do so, this catastrophe need not have occurred. Had the nation as a whole been taken into confidence the sense of alienation that the Sikh community is now suffering from need not have taken place. Finally, is it fair to place an entire minority community in the dock for the sins of a few and to divert attention of the country from the failings of the administration?

Myth and Reality

M V KAMATH

In the summer of 1979 I visited Punjab as a state guest. I was then editor of The *Illustrated Weekly of India* and was planning a special issue on Punjab and had been assured of the fullest cooperation. The state was then governed by an Akali-Janata coalition headed by Mr Prakash Singh Badal, a heavy-set man who seemed to have lost the art of smiling. His officials, however, were more than helpful and I could not have been received with more kindness and hospitality.

It was my first visit to Punjab and I was anxious to see as much as possible. Later I set down my impressions. I repeat them here to get my own bearings:

Punjab is not just a state. It is a state of mind. And Punjabis are more than a people. They function as a family, if a somewhat extended one. One suspects that it is the cohesiveness of Punjabis and their deep sense of identity with their soil that together have made Punjab what it is.

Today's Punjab is a far cry from the great Punjab of pre-Partition days. Though Hindus are a substantial minority, the present-day Little Punjab is for all practical purposes a Sikh state. But paradoxically; while the stress is on Punjabi and the Gurmukhi script, the largest paper in Punjab is the *Hind Samachar* printed in Hindi (circulation 65,000) and its youthful editor, Ramesh Chander, will not let anyone forget it. Similarly, while Sardarjis may swear by their mother tongue, the number of English medium schools is increasing.

Punjab has all the characteristics of West Germany – except cleanliness. Soon after Partition, the state was in a total mess. The towns and cities lay desolate, spattered with communal blood. Two of the five rivers, virtually all the canal system and some of the best land went to Pakistan.

Add to it the fact that Punjab has neither coal nor heavy industry nor oil. Yet in wheat yield per hectare the Punjabi farmer has beaten farmers in the United States, the Soviet Union, Canada and Pakistan. In rice yield he has bested China and plans to beat Japan as well. The motto is 'Can Do.' Of every 100 kg of rice, Punjab's contribution to the union government is 56 kg. Of every 100 kg of wheat the government buys, Punjab provides 63 kg. And this from a state that does not eat rice and treats it as something to be eaten when one is sick!

Some believe that Punjabi prosperity has been made possible by money coming from Sikhs living abroad. To a small extent, possibly. In Jullundur district alone, according to one report, Punjab National Bank has foreign exchange deposits worth Rs 270 crore. Punjabis want all that money to be used in Punjab for development purposes. They say it is all 'their' money. The Reserve Bank, however, is chary of liberalizing credit facilities. Punjabis resent this.

All that Punjab wants, Chief Minister Sardar Prakash Singh Badal told me over the breakfast table, is re-casting centre-state financial relations. That meant, he said, revision of the Gadgil formula, reduction in the indebtedness of the state to the centre, change in the pattern of the loan assistance from the World Bank and equitable sharing of market borrowing between the centre and the states. Mr Badal said that the plain fact was that Punjab had been financing its plan effort largely through its own resources and that he was unhappy with the declining trend of central plan assistance to Punjab. Finance Minister S. Balwant Singh explained that the debate on fiscal autonomy should not be confused with talk of separatism, because it had nothing to do with it. Akalis were not separatists.

Punjabis want textile mills to be set up in their state. Why should Punjabi cotton have to go to Maharashtra to be spun and woven and sold back to Punjab at a profit? This they call in their naivette, colonialism.

With the establishment of Haryana and Himachal Pradesh, Punjab is for all purposes a Sikh state and as important as Punjab government is, the Shiromani Gurdwara Prabandhak Committee (SGPC) is capable of displaying as much authority as the government itself. It is sometimes hard to find out where politics ends and religion begins. Jathedar Jeevan Singh was of the opinion that Sikhs wanted greater autonomy for the state so that they can aim at results without having to clear everything with Delhi.

No two communities could be more akin to each other than the Punjabi Hindus and Sikhs and no two communities could be more dissimilar in their attitudes and reactions. The Sikhs want an autonomous Punjab and the extremists among them agitate for a sovereign Punjab; the Hindus want the powers of the state further reduced.

The Sikhs have carried on a long struggle to secure for Punjabi the exclusive status of official language while the Hindus disown it. The Sikhs take pride in Punjabi culture; the Hindus dismiss it as folk culture.

The Sikh migrants look to Punjab nostalgically and retain their links with it. The Hindu migrants feel relieved to have been spared the tensions of Akali politics. For the Punjabi

Hindus the heroes are not the Sikh gurus who were themselves originally Hindus, but Maharana Pratap and Shivaji. The Punjabi Hindus, at once unorthodox and conservative, are more concerned about Hindu identity than about Hindu ritual.

I was told that between the Punjabi Sikh and the Punjabi Hindu there was a conflict of culture. The problem had been complicated by the Partition of India, notably of Punjab. Both Hindus and Sikhs had to flee West Punjab. A majority of the Sikh refugees were accommodated in the Indian Punjab on the land left behind by the Muslims. But there was not much room for the Hindu refugees. The trades and professions in which they specialized were already crowded with Indian Punjabi Hindus. Moreover, the Hindu refugees, scorched by the divisive politics of the Muslims, wished to be settled away from the separatist politics of the Akalis. Happily for all, the Punjabi Hindu refugees posed no problem to their host states. They made no special demands for their language and culture. They adopted the language of their hosts and tried to identify themselves with it. This adjustment was the result of their conditioning in pan-Hinduism as against territorial patriotism. One writer told me: 'But what has helped Punjabi Hindus outside Punjab is proving to be a problem for them in Punjab. They do not accept the regional languague, Punjabi. They want Hindi instead. As long as Haryana remained a part of Punjab, Punjabi, of course, could not be the sole official language. But when, in 1966, the Hindi-speaking areas were separated and Punjab became a unilingual state, the Hindus left in Punjab felt orphaned. There is still no peace for the Punjabi Hindus. And there will be no peace for them until the Sikhs, conditioned to respond to the stimulus of a sovereign Sikh state, relent.'

One would have imagined that perfect amity would prevail between Hindus and Sikhs, considering that they come from almost the same stock. Most of the Sikh gurus had been originally Khatris. Of the nine gurus who followed Nanak, the first five had given spiritual strength and the last five had reinforced Hinduism with armed might. One publicist told me that tragedy struck Punjab the day when the Sikh Sabha, which had been formed to defend Sikhism against Christian attacks, declared that the Sikhs were not Hindus. For years, the Hindus in Punjab had to face Islamic efforts at conversion. Later still, challenges had come from the Christian missionaries. Then, to be disowned by Sikhs who were flesh of their flesh and blood of their blood was hard for Hindus in Punjab to bear. Their reaction was to seek strength in pan-Hinduism. But no encouraging response was forthcoming from the Hindus elsewhere in India which found the Congress better suited to their interests. The Congress based its politics on territorial patriotism. According to this, India had no religious communities, only linguistic groups. And ultimately this was to prove to be the nemesis of Hindus in Punjab. Either they accepted Punjabi as their language and stayed on in Punjab playing second fiddle to Sikhs who had disowned them, or they once again left their hearths and homes to find a place for themselves in the Hindi belt, in a second and even more traumatic migration. Was that possible?

At the Golden Temple where I was received with great respect, I was presented with a set of books by the Dharam Prachar Committee of the SGPC which I read with much interest and fascination. It included *Heritage of Sikh Culture* by Pritam Singh Gill, a former principal of Lyallpur Khalsa College, Jullundur. It was an eye-opener to me. I quote from it:

'Sikhs have their own culture quite distinct from that of other people inhabiting the rest of India. Their religious beliefs differ; their heritage *differs; so* their culture *differs...*

'In Bharat, the new India (after Partition) the concept of nationalism has remained the same in the minds of the Hindu community because they have connected language with religion even now. Hindi has been considered to be a language of all Hindus *irrespective of the region they live* in (emphasis added).

For them Hindi is the national language. They want to impose their language, religion and culture on the minority communities directly or indirectly. *They want to kill their cultures and make India a mono-cultural state.* In reality, they are after will-of-the-wisp. India would never have one culture, but this has been the tendency in the post-Partition period. Nationalism has been connected with Hindi, Hinduism and Hindu culture. This would certainly lead to a revolt and it may culminate in further disintegration of the country. The old definition of nationalism requiring community of language, religion and culture does not suit the Indian conditions. India being a multi-lingual, multi-racial, multi-religious and multi-cultural country, a new concept of composite nationalism will have to be evolved. This is a problem before the country ...

'The Sikhs have a history; they have a home; they have traditions; they have a well-developed language; they have a religion; they have a distinct society, morality and aesthetics. Thus they have a separate culture which they want to protect...'

Mr Gill devoted a whole chapter to show that Sikhs have been 'Victims of Hindu Nationalism'. As he put it: 'Indians got freedom, but not the Sikhs. Hindus left the enemy country and migrated to a country of their brothers. So did the Muslims. But the Sikhs left the enemy country and migrated to (another) enemy country. Out of frying pan they fell into fire. They were made to choose between two evils.' Mr Gill wrote: 'Kill the language, kill the culture, kill the community is the triple precept of Hindu diplomacy. This would make India mono-lingual, mono-cultural and mono-religious, they claim. This is the dream of Hindu nationalists... Any non-Hindi speaking man who declared his mother tongue as Hindi, became a hero; it was a simple method; it required telling a lie only. Hindus of the Punjabi-speaking area in Punjab told the biggest collective lie, when, at the time of census of 1951, all of them declared en bloc, that their mother tongue was Hindi and not Punjabi... Consequently, Punjabi was not given the status of full official and administrative language till 1966 and even after the reorganization of Punjab, it is being recognized half-heartedly and in the manner that it may die ultimately. At every step an attempt is made to place Hindi by its side. This is the position of a language which has been recognized as one of the regional languages in the constitution. This is with regard to Punjabi as a medium of administration.

'As regards the medium of instruction, an organized attempt is made to kill it. It has been left to the sweet choice of parents to decide about it. All Hindu institutions adopt Hindi as the medium; only the Sikh institutions take to Punjabi. In the government institutions there is a partition on a small scale, into Hindi-speaking student community and Punjabi-speaking student community. In the former, Hindus are predominant and in the latter, Sikhs. This partition is the making of Hindus and not the Sikhs...

'The crux of the problem is that Hindus do not want to be dominated by any other community in any state (province) because they are the ruling race... They are Hindus first and then Indians...The cultural minorities are at the mercy of their voting power, therefore, they are in search of some means of protecting their culture: they don't want to be absorbed. They need safeguards for the protection of their cultures. So there are two distinct tendencies, centripetal and centrifugal. This clash would remain as long as India lives in the past, especially the majority community. The attitude of the minority communities is a reaction against the behaviour of the majority community whose rights are now beyond any danger. For the minorities, it is a question of life and death. So it is up to the majority community now to change the concept of nationalism and not the minority communities...'

Mr Gill went to great lengths to show that Sikhs, somehow, are different from, and not to be confused with, Hindus. Mr Gill did not quite go to the extent of saying that Sikhs must have a separate state, but the trend of his argument was clear.

Since his book was presented to me by the SGPC, I would imagine that it approves the general trend of Mr Gill's argument.

In his chapter on the politico-cultural history of Punjab, Mr Gill clinched his argument thus:

'It is useless to assert that India has one culture. Diversity is there nobody can deny but some say that there is unity in diversity This is nothing but self-deception and a wishful thinking of the few.

Is there any unity of the religious teachings of Hinduism, Jainism, Buddhism, Islam, Sikhism and Zoroastrianism? No, their fundamentals differ.

Is there any unity of language, race and heritage? No.

How many people marry out of their religion? They can be counted on fingers.

How many people are untouchables? Millions.

Have people shed their prejudices of food and dress? No.

How many are considered to be second rate citizens? The majority community can tell.'

The gist of Mr Gills' theorizing is that India never was one, never can be one and therefore never should be one.

One would presume that because Mr Gill's book is distributed by the Dharam Prachar Committee of the SGPC, it reflects the thinking of the SGPC. But does the SGPC reflect the sentiments of all Sikhs? We do not know and cannot tell, short of holding a referendum in Punjab.

I remember how shocked and sad I felt when I read Mr Gill's book for the first time. Sad, not because Mr Gill attacked Hinduism, or that he gave a perverted view of the development of Hindu society, but that anybody, in this day and age, would want to be an alien in his own land.

When I re-read the book in the context of recent events, I began to wonder whether it could just be that a substantial majority of Sikhs feel like him, even if they do not want a Khalistan or Sikhistan.

In the long history of Punjab there never was a time – except for a brief period of fifty years – when Sikhs ruled the area. The concept of Punjab itself has changed over the centuries, if not decades. The concentration of Sikhs in Indian Punjab is the result of an historical accident. The Sikhs as a people themselves have a history of not more than 300 years. If one is strictly to go by history, Khalistan should include Pakistan Punjab as well with Lahore as its capital. And in a Khalistan, are Sikhs going to make it mandatory for all non-Sikhs to learn Punjabi against their will? And is it expected that all Sikhs outside Khalistan should be treated as second-class citizens, unworthy of being trusted? Somewhere, logic comes apart in a welter of emotions.

The creation of Pakistan has had its own trauma among Muslims left behind in India. The burden of their complaint is that they are now being treated as second-class citizens. Should a Khalistan come about, how are the Sikhs in the Indian Army to be treated: as mercenaries? Or is it expected that they are disbanded and sent to a mythical Khalistan? And is it further expected once again to exchange populations with Sikhs living in India repatriated to Khalistan and such Hindus as now living in today's Punjab repatriated to a residual India? How ridiculous can one be?

One of the major tragedies of India is that we have come to associate parts of the country with a particular language and the people who speak the language as separate from others who don't. Linguistic states have been the bane of post-Independence, neither during the British period nor during the reigns of numerous kings and queens. The Maratha empire encompassed lands where many languages were spoken. The Vijayanagara empire included both Telugu and Kannada areas. Language was never a problem. The poisonous seeds of linguism were sown by the Congress and the public is now reaping the fruits.

Interestingly enough, the situation in Punjab has a parallel in – of all places in Goa. During the time of the Portuguese rule, when the local language, Konkani, was under seige, Hindus determinedly stuck to it, while it became fashionable for the upper crust of Catholics to discard it in favour of Portuguese. Konkani had no status in its own homeland. Goan Hindus making their livelihood in Bombay would more often give Marathi, the dominant language of the region, as their mother tongue in order to associate themselves with the dominant group and thereby to get such crumbs from the dominant group's table as became available.

When the Portuguese were finally driven out, the Catholics, who are in a minority in Goa, suddenly found themselves bereft of their patrons. To learn Portuguese was no more a paying proposition; it did not set them apart as the ruling class. On the contrary, it showed them somewhat sharply as an alien minority. But never having associated themselves with the Marathi dominant group, they could not now claim Marathi as their mother tongue. Their salvation lay in asserting themselves as Konkani-speaking people. But this new-found love for Konkani had become suspect, besides which the majority Hindus having sought favour from the dominant group and received it were now reluctant to acknowledge publicly that Konkani was their mother tongue, even though they spoke the language at home! The Hindu-Catholic cleavage in Goa remains sharp with the Goan Hindus, like the Punjabi Hindus who claim Hindi as their mother tongue, claiming Marathi as their own, even though, unlike the Punjabi Hindus in Punjab, they are the majority in Goa. Though the Hindus were – and remain – the majority community in Goa, for five centuries they had remained out of power and behaved like a minority. Their association with Marathi was instinctive and security-related. This is in the nature of life itself. Had the Sikhs been in a minority in Punjab, the Hindus probably would have had less inhibitions in claiming Punjabi as their mother tongue. The Catholics in Goa alienated the Hindus linguistically; without probably meaning to, the Sikhs in Punjab have alienated their Hindu brothers. There is somewhere, here, an object lesson. When language is associated with power, it assumes highly emotive connotations.' When language and religion get linked, the mixture can become explosive. If Goa has not exploded it is merely because Christianity had a sobering influence on the people, the Goans besides, being themselves a sober people given to literature, music, theatre and the arts and not to sabre-rattling. Compromises come easily to them.

It is also understood that while Konkani is a beautiful language, it has no great market value as compared to Marathi; much the same can be said of Punjabi or for that matter Oriya or Assamiya; they are beautiful languages full of meaning and nuances to those who speak them but on an all-India level, they cut little ice. Those who want to stir out of their linguistic nests learn quickly enough that while it is highly patriotic to swear by one's mother language, it is more practical to learn a dominant language. Punjabi may be spoken by as many as 35 per cent of the people in Haryana and yet not recognized as a second language, but there surely is a method in that madness. Punjabi has no all-India future; Hindi has. So, even though Punjabi is the first language in Punjab, it has perforce to make Hindi the second language, and while this may be attributed to large-heartedness of the Sikhs, one may suspect some pragmatism in the generosity as well. In 1973 India made 147 films in Hindi, 5 films in Punjabi, 2 in Oriya and 8 in Assamese and none in Konkani. In that same year there were 255 dailies, and 1,595 weeklies published in Hindi while there were only 18 dailies and 104 weeklies in Punjabi. Hindi has a bigger clout. Hindi, as Sikhs should know, is officially discouraged in Tamil Nadu whose first language, Tamil, is reputed to be older than Sanskrit. And yet Hindi is being taught in many schools if only because the enterprising Tamilian wants to be able to make a living elsewhere in India. If the Sikh is a little less jingoistic about Punjabi, he will be more at peace with himself and his

Hindu brothers. Language is important, but not that important to wreck inter-communal peace.

There are four strands to Punjab crisis fabric that need to be understood. One is the religious strand; the second is the language strand; the third is the terrorist strand and the fourth, and probably the most vicious, is the political strand. The language strand is easily disposed of. Religious tensions are of a recent vintage. Whether Sikh leadership wishes to assert a separate Sikh identity or not, there has been a long history of close Hindu-Sikh relationship. Guru Teg Bahadur's unparalleled sacrifice of his head to protect the sacred thread and the forehead mark of the Hindus is a matter of record. So is the fact that Maharaja Ranjit Singh banned cow slaughter not only in Punjab but even ordered its ban in Afghanistan and secured the return of the doors of the temple at Somnath looted eight centuries earlier by Ghazni Mohammad. The universally applicable scriptures of the Sikhs incorporate, as is well-known, many hymns from 'Hinduism' and the names recognized by Hindus, such as Ram, Hari, Govind, Gopal, Siva, Brahma and Indra are repeated in the Adi Granth time and again. There is one school of thought which says that there is no such thing as Hindu-Sikh clash and point out that despite all the provocations in recent times there has not been one significant communal riot in Punjab and that in village after village, the Hindu minority has been protected by the Sikh majority.

There is another school of thought which argues that there are tensions between the Sikhs and the Hindus, but that this cannot be attributed to Hindus as such, the reasons being attributable to the Arya Samajists and as witness thereof are lines from *Satyartha Prakash* written by Swami Dayananda Saraswati, that are derogatory to the Sikh gurus. At the same time it is a well-known fact that those who worship at the shrines of the gurus include large numbers of Hindus.

If there are sharp and cognizable differences between the Sikhs and the Hindus (or to be more specific, Arya Samajists) who created them? The Sikhs? The Hindus? The British? For surely, these are not the handiwork of Mrs Gandhi, Pakistan or the CIA? And equally surely, Hindus living away from Punjab could have had no hand in creation of the schisms?

In Punjab, one can never be sure who really set in motion the trend toward Sikh separatism. The Arya Samajists may lay the blame at Sikh doors and the Sikhs may point the finger at the Arya Samajists, and the argument can go on endlessly, but it does seem that at some stage, a sizeable section of Sikhs had come to feel that a largely autonomous state under Sikh domination would be their advantage. If they gave any thought to how their Hindu brothers would feel, it does not come through.

Talk of autonomy ceased when the Akalis came to power with the aid of the BJP. But every time the BJP rescued Akalis, there would be a swing of Hindu votes to Congress-I, and it would be the BJP that lost. But the last rule of Congress-I under Darbara Singh proved ephemeral. Some say he was spending most of his time fending off central interference, from Zail Singh, Buta Singh and others. But Congress-I rule also saw heightened terrorism. The conventional argument is that there was a lot of counter-terrorism practised under the Darbara regime and that this alienated a large number of Sikhs who thereafter went to the Bhindranwale camp. It will never be easy to find out the rights and wrongs of the situation.

It is dangerous, in a highly volatile state, to practise the game of Divide and Rule as did Mrs Indira Gandhi. Punjab has certain characteristics unique to it. It is a border state. It is adjacent to Jammu and Kashmir, which is another border state and with whose leaders Mrs Gandhi has been in a state of permanent conflict. It is a farily well-knit state with a majority of the people bound together by the ties of religion that have no parallel anywhere else in the world. There is certainly no other state in India where a people can be rallied round one temple, one source of inspiration and one concept: in this case, the uniqueness of the Sikh people. The internal disputes and dissensions among the Sikh people are best left for them to resolve without external interference. Any central interference will leave the interferer – in this instance Mrs Gandhi – open to the charge that she is working against the interests of the entire Sikh people. One political commentator and analyst has already described central intervention in Punjab as 'a war against the Akali party.' The worst thing that can be done to Punjab is to split the Sikhs or to pitch them against the Hindus. Whatever their problems, whether intra-Sikh, or Sikh-Hindu, are best left for the Sikhs and the Hindus to resolve among themselves. To sow conflict in Punjab in the hope of maintaining Congress-I supremacy in the state, as Rajni Kothari has accused the party of doing, is to invite trouble. This is not to argue, as Mr Kothari has done, that the genesis of the trouble in Punjab is Mrs Gandhi's overweening desire to maintain Congress-I 'the only moral principle in politics.' This is to turn a blind eye to many factors that have contributed to the crisis that emerged in Punjab. If one must look to the root cause of trouble one must rather go to the setting up of linguistic states which has aroused deep passions. Shakespeare makes one of his characters, Glendower say (King Henry IV) with conviction: 'I can call spirits from the vast deep' to which Hotspur replied: 'Why, so can I, or so can any man; but will they come when you do call for them?' In India, with the establishment of linguistic states, these spirits are surfacing on their own. And they spell danger to the nation.

A warning against such an eventuality was sounded as recently as 17 August 1963 by C. Rajagopalachari (Rajaji). He then wrote: 'The multilingual provinces of the old regime were developing synthesis each within its own wide boundaries of more than one language community tending towards an all-India synthesis. The unfortunate linguistic reorganization of states on a single-language basis stopped this process of synthesis. The states have hardened into rigidly isolated units developing a language nationalism with a proprietary ego and an aggressive attitude towards one another. All India unity is badly affected by this. The binding factor is the central government, namely, the image of the illustrious emancipators from foreign rule which is thining and is bound to vanish and leave India in a state of disintegration, state nationalism replacing all-India nationalism. Increased power for the centre is not a remedy, as some people believe. It will not help to build but only serve to provoke rebellion. This will be so because the centre will always be identified with the stronger state or group. This is a gloomy picture though distant' (emphasis added).

Rajaji's prophecy has come to pass now in Punjab. His assessment was correct. Mrs Gandhi has been functioning on the theory, amounting to a deep-seated belief, that only a powerful centre can serve as a binding force. The force that in the early years of post-independence India kept the country together was not so much central authority, or even the charisma of Jawaharlal Nehru, but 'the image of the illustrious emancipators from foreign rule'. With the thining out of that image, and with the wrong step that the nation took in establishing linguistic states, it was inevitable that the 'increased power' sought by the centre should only arouse 'rebellion'. In that sense the answer to our problems, whether in Punjab or elsewhere, is the dissolution of the linguistic states and the setting up of a unitary republic.

When Rajaji made his remarks, his motives were suspect. He was condemned for wanting to retain English as the inter-state language. Rajaji did hold that view strongly. He said: 'All our languages are great and good and sacred. (But) do not seek to elevate one of them over others. Let the official service continue to be done in English as heretofore. This is the simple key to the problem that has raised its head. It is my earnest advice as an old and experienced citizen of India who is not less patriotic than anyone else in this great country of ours, and who yields to none in love and respect for Indian institutions, Indian manners and customs and Indian languages.'

The occasion was the demand for making Hindi 'the national language' of India. In Tamil Nadu, Rajaji's home state, the demand was opposed with a vehemence that should have been foreseen, but which the Hindi-belt majority in parliament, in its blindness, refused to see. Language is a powerful force. It should not have been summoned from the deep. In any event, it should not have been associated with political power. Its worst manifestation has been seen in Punjab, where it has created an explosive mix of language, religion and politics. No deadlier combination exists. The three have to be separated, but the process must start elsewhere in the country. We must either get back to the old multilingual provinces or, if that is not feasible, to a unitary form of government where India is divided into 450 districts with no linguistic tag attached to them.

Were India a unitary state, divided not into linguistic states, but into several districts, some of the demands made by the Akali Dal just would not have arisen, and the Anandpur Sahib Resolution would have been a piece of paper. When Rajaji spoke of 'proprietary ego' he pinpointed the problem accurately. The Akalis speak of rivers in Punjab as if they are their exclusive property whose waters can be shared by others only through their courtesy. Maharashtrians and Gujaratis, Kannadigas and Tamilians not to speak of people from other states talk of the Narmada or the Kaveri as if they are theirs by natural right. Maharashtrians, similarly, demanded that the city of Bombay is theirs, forgetting that it has been the handiwork of generations of people who spoke a language other than Marathi. In a unitary state no problem of river waters can arise since water will be used not by states but by people who live by the rivers. Cities like Delhi, Calcutta, Madras, Bombay would be treated as units in their own right and not as capitals of any particular state. In fact, when the old Bombay province was to be trifurcated, there was a positive and entirely sensible proposal to make Bombay a centrally-administered unit. But such was linguistic jingoism that threats came to be issued that if Bombay was taken away from Maharashtra, it would be starved of water. In the end, the centre was compelled to succumb to the demands of the jingoists.

During the linguistic agitation in 1953, over 50,000 Sikhs had courted arrest. In the 1983 agitation, reputedly over 100,000 volunteers similarly offered themselves for arrest, in a sheer exercise in futility. Chauvinism of the worst kind had run riot. The mountains and rivers, the vales and forests, the seas and beaches of this ancient land belong to all people. They are not – and should not be – the sole property of any group, whether religious or linguistic.

It is because this sound principle had been thrown overboard by all concerned that there has been so much bad blood between one state and another. So-called leaders in every state have now come to have vested interests in prolonging and maintaining linguism in determining political units. Is there any wonder, then, that Sikhs, too, want to have their Punjab suba? And who can blame them for complaining that they were the last to get their own Punjabi-speaking state, long after other linguistic units had been established? And once you start accumulating grievances, they have a way of getting out of hand. Grievance piles up on grievance until one convinces onself that the world is against one. In Punjab, the Akalis seem to have convinced themselves that every hand is turned against them, that there is a diabolical conspiracy to do the Sikhs out of their heritage and to turn them into second-class citizens. That will partly explain the Anandpur Sahib Resolution, the frustrations expressed by many Sikh leaders and the ease with which Sikhs could be made to think that they have to make it on their own.

Then comes self-pity, a feeling that one's contributions to the nation have gone unrecognized, that one is victim of circumstances beyond one's control and that one's destiny is in one's own hand. Sant Longowal, for instance, told a visiting delegation that out of 2,125 martyrs, as many as 1,550 (or 75 per cent) were Sikhs, that out of 2,646 deported to Andaman (*Kalapani*), 2,147 (80 per cent) were Sikhs and that out of 127 Indians who were sent to the gallows, 92 (or 80 per cent) were Sikhs. The Sant also pointed out that in Netaji Subhas Chandra Bose's Indian National Army of 20,000, almost 12,000 were Sikhs. Thus, complained the Sant, not only did India's 2 per cent Sikhs make by far the highest contribution to the country's freedom, but they also maintained the same tempo even after India became free. More than one third of the country's population, he added, lived on the grain produced and supplied from Punjab which was a deficit state with its barren lands at the time of Partition.

There is no doubt that the better irrigated lands of Punjab went to Pakistan. Equally, there is no doubt that the Green Revolution in India was mostly the handiwork of the Punjabi Jat farmer, hardy, innovative and enterprising. Mr C. Subramaniam has gone on record as saying that it was the Punjab farmer with his willingness to experiment who made the Green Revolution possible, though the Tamil Nadu farmer, it has to be added, was soon to follow suit. The Sant's argument has been that the central government's investment in the Green Revolution has been less than one per cent of the national budget though, if one were to look into statistics more carefully, one would learn that central investment in the Green Revolution was not much more elsewhere, either.

The point can be made, of course, that the Punjabi farmer has not been giving his grain free and that by now he must have reaped several times the investment that he had made and that if the Punjabi farmer or small-scale industrialist has been thriving it is because of the great market he enjoys and the rest of India provides. Many states in India even provide labour to Punjab, though Punjab, in turn, can claim that it is putting money into the pockets of labourers from Bihar, Uttar Pradesh and Rajasthan who would otherwise have remained unemployed and to that extent poorer. What needs to be stressed here, of course, is that all states are highly interdependent and it is that which makes India so fascinating a land to live in.

Indeed, it is not only that non-Punjabi labour goes every year to Punjab to work on the farms but that Punjabis themselves have fanned out all over India to make an honourable living. According to the 1981 census there are 101,762 Sikhs in Maharashtra, 98,973 in Madhya Pradesh, 105,873 in Jammu and Kashmir, 61,520 in Bihar, 44,914 in Himachal Pradesh, 35,084 in West Bengal, 12,591 in Andhra Pradesh, 11,920 in Assam, 18,233 in Gujarat, 10,284 in Orissa, 6,830 in Karnataka, 4,355 in Tamil Nadu and 292,123 in Delhi. There are more Sikhs in Delhi than in Amritsar.

But it would be unwise and factually erroneous to think that Punjab, the granary of India, has brought plenty and prosperity to the state. That is a wrong assumption. It is true that the farmers in Punjab are owners-cultivators, but 48.44 per cent of the farming households have small holdings of less than five acres each and together own only 13.13 per cent of the land, while 41.56 per cent own 49.79 per cent of the area. A major section of the land – 37.08 per cent – is held by the remaining 10 per cent. Each household in this category owns 20 acres or more. As Jagtar Singh has pointed out in *Express Magazine* (22 July 1984), the majority of small-holders – 45 per cent of the population of the state, according to the latest government surveys – lives below the poverty line. That is a frightful thought.

A close study of the facts reveals that the fruits of the Green Revolution have been reaped largely by the top 10 per cent of the owner-farmers like Prakash Singh Badal, former chief minister of Punjab. A World Bank study had warned of increasing social tensions caused by this kind of lopsided development, but apparently this has not been taken seriously.

The socio-economic profile of Punjab is fairly frightening. The number of cultivators pushed out of the land-owning classes was stated to be 7 per cent between 1961-71. Again, the area tilled by each agricultural labourer fell from 2.23 hectare in 1961 to 1.75 hectares in 1981. As Jagtar Singh noted, the real wages of agricultural labour also fell while its ranks swelled, with marginal farmers pushed out due to economic compulsions.

As with the rural areas, so with urban unemployment. The number of professionals and technically trained youth on the live register of the employment exchanges increased, unbelievably, from a mere 9,321 in 1966 to 64,771 in 1981. The number of those seeking clerical, white-collar jobs increased from 2,713 in 1966 to 45,708 in 1981 and the total number of those unemployed increased from 50,578 to 486, 081 during the same period. The picture becomes more alarming if one were to take note of the fact that not all who are unemployed register their names nor do those who are partially employed or underemployed.

Another painful fact has emerged from recent studies. This is that the average growth rate in terms of value added has been lower than the output, a situation which, incidentally, a Western farmer is aware of. The unwritten truth about the Green Revolution is that once growth rate depends upon steady provision of fertilisers and chemicals, the input/output ratio comes into operation. In Punjab, that has meant that only those farming households that have enough marketable surplus and the capacity to hoard have benefitted from the Green Revolution.

Another aspect of Punjab's economy which has been partly responsible for the 'persecution complex' of the Punjabis is that, he is the biggest consumer of finished goods. It is stated that more liquor, for example, is consumed in Punjab than even in Maharashtra and Maharashtrians are no slouches when it comes to drinking. And yet, apparently, Punjabis drink more, quantity-wise and per capita than any other people in the rest of India. This means that unknowingly, money is siphoned off from Punjab to other states.

All these facts, coupled with the natural militancy of the Sikhs, have contributed to the growth of violence which has been exploited by various political groups. It is well to remember that since 1947 there have been three militant movements in Punjab, with the cycle repeating itself every ten to fifteen years. The first movement was led by Teja Singh Swatantra, in the then Patiala and East Punjab States Union (PEPSU) immediately after Independence and is credited with success in getting ownership rights to tenant cultivators. In fact, it is said, the first Tenancy Act in the state was passed by the PEPSU government under the pressure of Teja Singh's Lal Party.

The second movement coincided, interestingly enough, with the advent of the Green Revolution after the birth of Naxalism in West Bengal, in 1967. It spluttered to an end five years later in 1972, but not before it claimed the lives of eighty-five people, including two heroes of the Independence movement, Baba Buzha Singh (85) and Baba Hari Singh Margind (70). The movement was crushed because it did not have a mass base.

The current – and third – movement comes in the wake of a decade and a half of the making of the Green Revolution, with the polarization of classes. One assessment is that most of those who joined Bhindranwale were those left behind by the Green Revolution.

The situation was ripe. In the first place, many scapegoats were available to hang the peoples' frustration on. The peasants and landless labour invariably were Sikhs. But if the means of production were in the hands of the Sikhs, the marketing and distribution of produce was in the hands of the Hindus who could always be dubbed the exploiters.

Then there was the central government which had put a brake on Akali ambitions to monopolize patronage, and distribute the fruits of office. The Akalis could always say that, but for the centre – a euphemism for Mrs Gandhi – they would have provided more jobs and more employment opportunities to the people, forgetting the fact that most of the exploiters were the rich Sikh landlords themselves.

But the anger against domestic exploiters was easy to deflect with a fundamentalist like Bhindranwale breathing fire and brimstone on the scene. He had his own devils to excoriate, like modernism, heresy and westernization. An unsophisticated farmer's son, he had earlier been unscrupulously used by Congress-I power brokers to break the back of the Akali agitators who had their own axe to grind. Once, largely because of Congress-I fumbling, Bhindranwale felt that he could be a power unto himself, he began to attract all the elements in Punjabi society that had a grievance: the lumpen proletariat, the ex-Naxalites trying to re-group, plain criminals, smugglers and dregs of society, wide-eyed idealists who felt that Khalistan was the answer to their economic and social problems and so on. The stage was set for a denouement.

The Sikhs had for long wanted to have a separate state where they could be the overlords but their case had always been weak. Lord Louis Mountbatten had pointed out that since in no district in the original Punjab had the Sikhs a majority, 'it is out of the question to meet their claims by setting up a separate Sikh state'. 'The Sikhs,' he added, 'have an exaggerated idea of their proper status in the future setup.'

This had been galling to Sikh pride. The Anandpur Sahib Resolution was the formulation of Sikh frustration and anger. According to the Resolution, 'the Sikhs have been politically recognized as a political nation ever since the inauguration of the Order of the Khalsa in the concluding year of the 17th century.' So, it was argued, the Shiromani Akali Dal 'proclaims that the Sikhs are determined by all legitimate means to extricate and free themselves from the degrading and death-dealing situation so as to ensure finally their honourable survival and salvage their inherent dignity and their brithright to influence meaningfully, the mainstream of the world history.'

Towards that end, according to the Anandpur Sahib Resolution, 'the Sikhs therefore demand, firstly that an autonomous region in the north of India should be set up forthwith wherein the Sikh interests are constitutionally recognized as of primary and special importance as the public and fundamental state policy!'

The Resolution added: 'This Sikh autonomous region may be conceded and declared as entitled to frame its own constitution on the basis of all powers to and for itself except foreign relations, defence and communications to remain as subjects with the federal government.'

And what were to be the geographic dimensions of this Sikh autonomous state? The Anandpur Sahib Resolution is pretty clear on that. According to it, Khalistan would include 'present Indian Punjab, Karnal and Ambala districts of Haryana inclusive of Kangra district and Kulu Valley of Himachal Pradesh comprised in Paonta Saheb, Chandigarh, Pinjore, Kalka, Dalhousie, Dehra Doon Valley, Nalagarh Desh, Sirsa, Guhla and Rattia areas and Ganganagar district of Rajasthan and the Tarai region of the UP recently reclaimed and colonized by the Sikhs out of thousand-year-old virgin and dangerously infested forests, thus bringing the main contiguous Sikhs population and traditional and natural Sikh habitats still parts of and included in India, within this autonomous Sikh region.'

At no time did the Akalis repudiate the Anandpur Sahib Resolution and in the circumstances it makes little sense to try to differentiate between 'moderates' and 'extremists' within the Akali camp. The goal of both was the same: an independent Khalistan. And it is the repudiation of the Anandpur Sahib Resolution that must precede any future discussion with the Akalis, 'moderate' or 'extremists.'

Is it in the cards? Nobody can say. Terrorism, no doubt, will be contained in the course of time as the terrorists themselves see the futility of their ways or are fought to a standstill as happened in West Bengal or Andhra Pradesh. Earlier waves of terrorism have been put down and they surely will be put down this time, too, the Congress(I) government having learnt the error of its ways. But for the Akalis to formally repudiate the Anandpur Sahib Resolution would be a major step. And yet, without the repudiation of that resolution, no negotiation would be worthwhile. All other demands put forward by the Akalis from time to time, such as the transfer of Chandigarh, change in centre-state relations were mere tactical ploys floated by the Akalis to feel the ground for the ultimate goal. Even if the Government of India were to unilaterally grant them, it would be of no use because the main cause for all the tensions to date would not have been resolved. The main cause is the Anandpur Resolution and the demand for separate Sikh statehood. Such a statehood cannot be granted, not only because it is not in the power of the centre to gift it, but because granting it would be to write off the unity and integrity of India. That, surely, is not negotiable?

Once the Anandpur Sahib Resolution is repudiated and the Akalis swear by the unity of India, many windows would then get opened. But will the problem be solved? As long as this country is divided along linguistic lines, the Sikhs will continue to grumble and as long as we talk in terms of minorities, the Sikhs will consider themselves an exploited minority. Both the concept of majority-minority and of linguistic states have to be scrapped. As long as we continue to think in terms of minority and majority, there is no incentive for the minority to join the mainstream. Why should the so-called minorities bestir themselves to get along with their fellow citizens when it is more paying to retain a distinct identity of their own and to foist on the so-called majority a giant guilt-complex? One of the demands of the Akali Dal, incidentally, is the removal of the limit of two per cent in Sikh recruitment to the armed forces. About the time of Partition, the Sikhs constituted almost nine per cent of the armed strength of the country. Subsequently, in order to establish equity and fairness in the armed forces, the government set a limit of two per cent to Sikh recruitment. This has been taken as one more attempt to put the Sikhs down, which is a travesty of truth. As a matter of fact, we have it on the authority of Lt Gen S.K. Sinha (Retd.) that Sikhs had not even in recent times filled in the two per cent upper limit. Even as it is, there are as many as 1,50,000 Sikh jawans serving in the Indian Army which would suggest that as many homes have a steady, if small, income to fall back on. And again, while pensions, too, are low, there certainly is some money coming in. Considering that as many as 598.70 million people out of a total population of India of about 700 million have a per capita expenditure of less than Rs 1,200 per annum or about Rs 100 a month, Punjab cannot be doing all that badly. Of how many regions in India can it be said that some 1,50,000 men are on government payroll on a regular basis and that almost as many of them must be on pension? Surely not Gujarat, Orissa or West Bengal?

India is large enough for all peoples, whether Hindu, Muslim or Sikh. It is catholic enough to accept all as equals, though instances of inequality can always be pointed out. This is a country of minorities. There is no one majority one can rile against. Punjab is better off than many other states and Punjabis have much to be thankful for. The financial cake available to the centre is small and it has to be parcelled out as equitably and judiciously as possible among many claimants, not all of whom get a fair share. If only the Sikhs realize how lucky they are and have been, they would be more understanding of the problems of the centre. In any event, violence and terrorism are hardly the means to be adopted to get desirable goals. It will be claimed on behalf of the Sikhs that not all of them were involved in the recent events and that a good percentage of them abhor violence, of any kind. It is equally true that people do noten masse protest against violence, even if they be dead against it, for that is not in the nature of man. To that extent it would be right to say that the sins of Bhindranwale should not be visited upon all Sikhs, indiscriminately. For the government it can be said that it surely hasn't any intention of tarring all Sikhs with the same brush, but how is one to distinguish between a terrorist and an innocent citizen? The problem for the innocent citizen is compounded by the fact that should he reveal the whereabouts of a terrorist, he himself stands to be killed. That, clearly, was the dilemma of the Sikh intellectuals many of whom preferred to remain silent than be critical of the thugs who ruled from the Golden Temple premises.

Could the events in Punjab have been prevented? Hindsight shows us that they could have been. But we can now go only forward, not backward. The repair of the Akal Thakt, no doubt, will go on, whether by one or other group. This article has attempted to bring all the issues that have contributed to the breakdown of peace in Punjab in broad outline. No doubt more details could be filled in, especially the relations between Zail Singh and Bhindranwale and the role of Congress(I) in encouraging terrorism. But enough has been stated, one hopes, to show that nothing is as simple as it seems.

The Great Divide

SUNIL SETHI

In the summer of 1982 Jarnail Singh Bhindranwale was still an easily approachable, less-than-formidable figure. The Golden Temple was not yet an area cordoned off by fear and outrage. And Amritsar was a self-assured boom town, unaware that its life would so quickly be short-circuited by a reign of terror and retribution.

There were those, of course, who saw the government's organized, and highly publicized, surrender of Bhindranwale at Chowk Mehta as a dangerous signal. But there was no one to predict that he could be transformed into an all-powerful, malignant force. No one imagined that he could hold Punjab on a short fuse. At best, he was a dispensable pawn in a political game. At worst, a combination of half-clown, half-loon.

All day long, in those early days in Guru Nanak Niwas, he would lie on the rooftop, stretched out on a camp cot, his long black beard glistening in the sun and his eyes narrowing expectantly at the sight of visitors. These were few and far between: a straggle of journalists quizzing him about his dubious past or ambiguous present or groups of curious villagers who had struggled up the eight flights of stairs to view a man surrounded by recent controversy. In those days Bhindranwale was looking for visitors, especially those from the media. I remember how eager he seemed to please. Springing from his seat at the sight of a camera or notebook, he was all effusive, greeting and ordering glasses of cold water to be fetched. He showed all the nervousness and excitement of a man looking for attention; he seemed genuinely flattered that he was getting it. And there was little in his conversation, other than his railings against Nirankaris, that was provocative or incendiary. He stuck to long, rambling, disconnected sermons about the Sikh faith, delivered in the manner of a village preacher. Clouded as these were by a turn of phrase and metaphor so rustic, they were not exactly crowd-pullers in the city. Questioned a little explicitly about his alleged connection in the murders of the Nirankari leader Gurbachan Singh or Jullundur editor Lala Jagat Narain, he betrayed an awkward evasiveness. He was liable to fall silent or mumble non-commital comments under his breath. His chief source of information as far as the media was concerned seemed to be the *Akali Patrika*. And this was at a time when it was hard to get him to say anything against the Akali Dal chief, Sant Harchand Singh Longowal, or SGPC president, Gurcharan Singh Tohra, then counted as the heavy-weight Sikh leaders.

In the year that followed after that first encounter, I met Bhindranwale about a dozen times, occasionally for meetings that stretched over a whole morning or afternoon. In retrospect, it seems difficult to pinpoint on which visit precisely the transformation from a village preacher to national figure seemed discernible, just as it is difficult to say when the humble welcome turned into an arrogant swagger and, finally, into preemptory dismissals of journalists he did not wish to speak to. But I do recall instances, at least three, that give a fair example of his stiffening clout, his growing sophistication in handling the media and his hardening communal stance.

The first was in late 1982 when his anti-Nirankari tirade developed into anti-government and anti-Longowal onslaught. Imperceptibly at first, and blatantly later, the utterances became anti-Hindu. It is impossible to translate into English the particular venom with which these statements were delivered in a crude peasant's Punjabi or the obnoxious innuendos they were loaded with. It was as if Bhindranwale, with the arrival of every interviewer, was sharpening his invective to keep the presses turning. Each visit yielded sayings more inflammatory than the last. His favourite story, for example, of atrocities committed upon Sikhs by Hindus was the instance of a village near Moga where the Hindus had ganged up against a Sikh girl. 'She was harassed and then beaten,' he said, 'and then in full public view stripped naked. As if that was not enough, they (the Hindus) forced her father to have intercourse with her.' I heard him tell this story at least three times. And if at all times Hindus were not actually singled out as the aggressors, it was clear to the growing congregations, listening in rapt attention, who was. And if he did not actually specify the nature of the reported assault, the phrase he used in Punjabi was so suggestive that no one was in any doubt as to the implications of such a monstrous action. But when asked to furnish details of the name of the family, village, etc., Bhindranwale turned evasive and belligerent. 'I expect nothing but these foolish questions from you,' he snapped angrily at me once when I pressed him for details, 'if you were a Sikh you would be able to believe it.' It is only an indicator of the media's discretion that it repeatedly exercised restraint in reporting such stories.

Yet it was his consistent pandering to the media that was equally perverse. Being a heavy smoker I sometimes found my patience exercised by his hours of endless rhetoric. Sometimes I would slip away and drive out as far as the police station about a kilometre away to return after a cigarette break. He either noticed my absence or my breath gave me away, because he once conspiritorially asked me when there were not many people around, if I smoked. 'Yes,' I answered. 'Well,' he said grinning with his long, yellowing teeth, 'why don't you just go in that far corner and get it done with.' 'Mind you,' he shouted as I gratefully crept away, 'don't blow any smoke in Darbar Sahib's direction.'

If such were his spirit of accommodation, it was also true that he could be an altogether shrewd and successful schemer and calculatedly play hard to get. In April 1983, Raghu Rai, the photographer, and I were working on a magazine's cover story on Punjab. Our plan for the perfect cover picture was to somehow persuade the four Sikh leaders – Bhindranwale, Longowal, Tohra and former chief minister, Parkash Singh Badal – to pose together. Given Longowal and Badal's ill – disguised antipathy for Bhindranwale it was a tall order. Still, we persevered in our persuasion of Bhindranwale, with Raghu exposing yards of film to soften him to the suggestion. Finally, he acquiesced and himself fixed a time and place for the shot: he would arrive the following morning at 7 a.m. sharp on the roof of the Teja Singh Samundari Hall provided we could get the others to agree.

It was a difficult job to talk them into it but, obviously, the idea of the four Sikh leaders appearing together on the cover at a time when the dissensions in the leadership were being widely aired, was a scheme the political leaders thawed to. Provided, they said, that we had made sure that Bhindranwale would turn up. With messages being passed to him till late at night – and assurances received – Raghu and I returned to our hotel quite pleased at our little coup. The next morning there was a drizzle and the clouds refused to clear up, but early and eager for a unique picture we were waiting on the roof of Teja Singh Samundari Hall. One by one the three leaders – Longowal, Tohra and Badal – appeared and waited in the rain for

Bhindranwale's arrival. The already embarrassing prestige issue as to who would arrive before, Bhindranwale or Longowal, became more embarrassing as the minutes ticked by and the assembled leaders grew wetter in the rain. Eventually, Tohra, the only one with any clout in Bhindranwale's camp, sent two messengers one after the other to haul him out. Back came the message: there was no Bhindranwale in Guru Nanak Niwas. He had chosen the exact moment for going into Darbar Sahib for his morning darshan. After a drippy photo session, the leaders thankfully dispersed, but the sting of it was not lost on Longowal, especially after the cover appeared with a closeup of Bhindranwale looming upon the picture of the three leaders. When I next saw him to ask about his viewpoint on politics of the moment, he giggled nervously and said: 'What viewpoint? Go ask your friend next door for viewpoints. We are not worth much given the space we get on your cover. I mean, you shoved us all into the bottom of his beard.'

If Bhindranwale was pleased at the success of his manoeuvre, he did not show it. Incensed by quotations inside that betrayed his anti-Hindu feeling, he refused to speak till a taperecorder was switched on. By now, the thin congregations of the year before had swelled into a daily swarm. A *shamiana* had been erected to shade the people from the afternoon sun. A spanking new taperecorder faithfully recorded every word he uttered and the latest ultra-sensitive Sony microphones were being brandished by a vastly-expanded squad of armed men who checked visitors at each flight of stairs. Lying on the same camp cot, with his toes thrust out for devotees to touch as they came in, he quickly pocketed cash offerings himself. It was now more difficult than ever to carry a sane or rational conversation with him. He would bark short, hard answers if he felt up to it. Or simply turn his face away. The only remarkable things he said to me, in an irritated high-handed-fashion, was that 'whoever performed those great feats (the murders of the Nirankari leader and Lala Jagat Narain) deserves to be honoured by the Akal Takht ... If their killers came to me, I would weigh them in gold.' And some especially nasty jibes about Sikh Congress(I) politicians whom he called '*sarkari* Sikhs.' This was Bhindranwale approaching his prime: a saviour touched by divinity in the eyes of some or a raving fanatic preaching hatred in the view of others.

The Bhindranwale now emerging in the complex web of growing violence and intrigue was the skilled political operator and arsenal builder, unraveller of hit lists and lethal blackmail. His power grew proportionately with his myth. His myth, in turn, buttressed his dictat which ricocheted through the city, so that people in Amritsar speak of the period as the period of 'Bhindranwale's government.' Simultaneously grew his authority as a religious and administrative leader: there were those who saw him as the ultimate dispenser of justice, the final arbiter on affairs social and temporal. He presided over marriages and ruled on property disputes; there was no area of life that his brand of extremist violence did not cast its ominous shadow upon. 'It was as if he had hijacked the whole town,' explained the general secretary of the largest Hindu temple in Amritsar later.

Looking back, the astonishing fact about Bhindranwale's meteoric, if terrifying, rise is that it took him less than a year to accomplish. True, it was a multiplicity of factors, both intentional and inadvertent, that fanned the aura of his myth and prowess. But it was not only the centre's continuing policy of drift, the weakening credibility of the Akali leadership and the defunct institutions and disabled politics of Punjab that propelled Bhindranwale to the forefront. His evil genius lay in grasping every twist and turn of the shifting scenario and capitalizing on every error of judgement made during the government's negotiations with the Akalis.

Equally, it was his charismatic appeal, and what it came to stand for among sections of the Sikhs who identified with him and today deify him. It was his capacity to offer them an alternative system, however subversive and trigger-happy, in place of one that had failed to keep pace with the galloping progression and dynamism of the people of of Punjab's. His fatal flaw was that his religious, ethos and political ambition failed to accommodate the aspiration of nearly half Punjab population, which happens to be non-Sikh. In gathering Sikh grievances under the all-purpose umbrella of a Sikh religious revival, Bhindranwale further isolated Punjab's Hindus. He succeeded in communalizing a society already polarized by the ongoing Akali agitation of three years. And his reign of terror drove the wedge so deep that a completely secular, wholly integrated society became afflicted with deep-seated scars.

If Bhindranwale's method of striving towards Sikh aspirations (whatever their fluctuating demands) was bloody and vindictive, it is because his interpretation of Sikh history was that of an illiterate village zealot: it proved rigid, iconoclastic and myopic in a modern secular state. A brief foray into Sikh history may serve as an example that motivated Bhindranwale in the direction he took.

In 1607 when the sixth Sikh guru Hargobind took charge, he stood at the Akal Takht which he had established, and there he adopted two swords, one symbolizing spiritual power and the other temporal authority. He adopted regal paraphernalia and introduced martial traits among his followers. He issued *hukumnamas* among them and commanded them to bring arms and horses instead of cash offerings. It is with no hint of irony that one can locate the parallel in Bhindranwale: his move from Guru Nanak Niwas to the Akal Takht in December 1983 was not merely a move to safer ground. The symbolism of the guru's example was not lost on him. He too was combining his spiritual power with temporal authority. He too was campaigning among his followers to collect weapons as well as cash offerings. It was a brilliant populist move. It served to enhance his aura as a truly spiritual leader, someone beyond the arm of the law as well as a remarkable upholder of the guru's example.

Reactions to Bhindranwale today, specially in Amritsar, where his authority was most strongly felt, show the degree to which opinion is polarized along communal lines after the Operation Bluestar. While a denunciation of the army action is unanimous and unequivocal among Sikhs everywhere, there are few who can openly find fault with Bhindranwale or his tactics, even if they suffered at his hands.

His popularity, if anything, has grown in the wake of the 'sacrilege'. Sikh shopkeepers whose shops had been destroyed due to two nights of crossfire in bazaars like Maniaran, Papad Bazaar and Tarkhanan Gali which lie directly behind the Akal Takht, pinned the entire blame of the battle upon the government. Bhindranwale, on the other hand, was viewed as a great man, a deeply religious saviour or a martyr. Two weeks after the Operation, rumour gripped the entire city that he was alive: that he had escaped miraculously, that he was safely in Pakistan, that he would one day be resurrected. 'No one saw his last rites so it is difficult to believe he is dead,' said Shyam Singh, a prosperous trader in Papad Bazaar whose shop had been razed to the ground. 'People like us,' he continued, 'were very dependant on Sant Bhindranwale. On various occasions we visited him to sort out disputes and he always had time for us. He gave good advice. He was a man concerned about the problem of every Sikh.' Others, if they were willing to concede that he was dead, referred to him and his men as *shahids* or martyrs, thereby establishing their noble end in the tradition of Sikh gurus.

The wave of outrage among Sikhs was generally directed towards the government, but on occasions spilled over to encompass Hindus. The sense of hostility was evident in the most commonplace exchange of conversation. Coming out of the Golden Temple among the rush of first visitors on 25 June, I was walking along an excitable group of Sikh women, returning home after witnessing the devastation inside. I casually asked one of them what she thought about it. Bitterly turning upon me, she snapped: 'You should know. It's your raj.' Registering the insult aimed directly at a Hindu, I retorted: 'Not my raj. It's army raj.'

'Well,' she shot back sharply, 'the army belongs to Indira Gandhi and Indira Gandhi belongs to you lot. Go ask her what there is to see inside.'

In the Sikh mind, the reaction to the army action had discernably hardened into the following equation: the army belongs to the government and the government belongs to Hindus. The example of Hindu offensiveness most often quoted by Sikhs after the action was the fact that in some Punjab towns they had distributed sweets in celebration of Bhindranwale's extermination.

Further offence was felt either due to a lack of authentic information put out by government media, such as the All India Radio and Doordarshan, or lack of its reliability. Television viewers in curfew bound Amritsar, for instance, were not shown the extent of damage to the Golden Temple till 2 July, over three weeks after the Operation. During that period they were fed on fleeting glimpses of the temple or shots of the weapons seized inside so often, that the crass repetition reduced government's credibility further and heightened the hostility. As a result, the suggestion that the pile-up of arms found inside had probably been planted by the government to discredit Sikhs gained credence. The government media's reports of the narcotics hoard found inside the temple, which were later contradicted, was quoted as one example of the government's effort to malign Sikhs. Sources of information being limited in the weeks after the action (stringent censorship was imposed on local newspapers) the television viewing habits of Amritsar's population also became polarized: Sikhs generally gave greater credence to Pakistan television's slickly produced, carefully propagandist news bulletins while Hindus quoted from

Doordarshan reports. 'The government has been vindictive towards Sikhs,' said Sardar Atma Singh, acting president of the SGPC who was later arrested. 'On the one hand it has set the army upon us, and on the other they have silenced our voices through censorship.'

The Hindu reaction after the army action was one of palpable relief, as if a long-festering sore had at last been decisively and successfully cauterized. Hindus generally spoke to applaud the government decision and gave graphic accounts of Bhindranwale's excesses. 'It is as if we have found another life,' said Bawa Joginder Singh, a wholesale trader in woollens whose shop had been looted by an angry Sikh mob in November 1982 in Bazaar Ghanta Ghar, a stone's throw away from the main Golden Temple entrance. For two years, he said, people like him had been subjected to listen to daily indoctrination and anti-Hindu speeches on loudspeakers from Manji Sahib, a public hall on the verge of the Golden Temple. 'Listening to those speeches day in and day out, you could feel the poison brimming over. It was a calculated assault on Hindus and Hindu sentiments. Our status had been reduced to that of targets for shooting practice.'

His neighbour, a businessman called Pran Mehra who deals in nylon yarn, said that his business had been so badly affected in the past two years that he had almost stopped coming to the shop. 'My retail counter sales were down by 90 per cent. There were simply no customers. I had originally taken this office because I thought it would be such a convenient address, being close to the Golden Temple. I did not realize how quickly it would become a curse.' The curse, claimed Mehra, lay in the daily threat of Bhindranwale's men arriving to extort money. 'There was no way anyone could refuse. Only 45 days before the action, his men came to me and asked me to vacate the office because they wanted to use the building as a morcha. I just pulled the shutters down that evening and stayed away.' Another shopkeeper in the vicinity said that Hindu-Sikh relations, strained for two years, had deteriorated in the aftermath of the army action.' Today every Sikh feels let down and vengeful. One of my customers said to me, 'We'll see you in two or three months after the army leaves.'

Even moderate Hindu opinion is based on fear of a vengeful Sikh reaction when the army leaves Punjab. Satish Mahajan, a well-known textile mill owner whose family has been in business in the city for 32 years, says that 'it is a case of being once bitten, twice shy.' 'The army action is bound to have some reaction sooner or later. Citizens who have burnt their fingers once feel that such a reaction must be dealt with effectively. That can only happen if there is a massive overhaul in the civil administration. Or chaos will return once the army leaves.'

The sense of relief is as understandable among Hindus as the overriding anguish and anger among Sikhs. Primary among the scares the Akali agitation wrought for the Punjabi Hindu, traditionally the shopkeepers, traders and industrialists of Punjab, was economic. It was the threat of having to close shop indefinitely. Over fifty per cent of Amritsar's population of about six lakhs being Hindu, and the majority of them being merchants, they have been sitting in their shops for two years watching their business run aground. 'Even if we closed our shops, where would we go?' A textile trader in the city who had been there since Partition told me last year, 'People like us have been uprooted once. We had to flee our homes when Pakistan was created. We won't flee them a second time in our lives. We won't leave because Sikhs want Khalistan. This is our home and we will fight for it and die here.'

Such a threat, remote and intangible two years ago, became more and more perceptible as Bhindranwale's terror tactics gathered momentum. Their extreme phase began after he had shifted into the Akal Takht. As the killings and threats of violence became more wanton, and citizens saw for themselves or heard stories about the fortifications being built inside the

Golden Temple and the arms being collected, the forebodings were no longer hypothetical. Especially, as there were daily instances of people directly coming to harm.

Even if some of the specific instances of blackmail and extortion quoted in Amritsar today may be coloured by the fact that the fountainhead of fear is eliminated, some of the stories are worth recording because they come from sources whose integrity is unimpeachable. And also because they provide a record of what was a very harrowing time in the life of a once-prosperous city that came close to paralysis.

One businessman I know had his car stolen from under his nose in January 1984 while his family visited an ice-cream parlour on Lawrence Road, a popular thoroughfare in the city. He said it was futile to raise an alarm because the men who drove away in the car were armed. And although a crowd collected, policemen on patrol duty were approached and later the theft registered, nothing happened. For months afterwards the owner heard reports of his car in use in the city – even the number plates had not been changed – and himself saw it twice. 'There was nothing I could do despite repeated protests to the police. It was a write off and I was advised to forget it.' Another businessman, a Delhi-based building contractor, who won an important public works tender for construction in Amritsar reported that days after work had started, he began to receive anonymous letters demanding a 'contribution' of Rs 50,000. If the money was not immediately handed over at a certain address by a certain time, the letters threatened kidnapping one of his family members. When next the contractor visited Amritsar he travelled under an assumed name and checked into a hotel incognito. Two days after his return to Delhi, he received a letter giving exact details of his subterfuge and demanding the delivery of cash promptly, failing which the kidnap would be effected. 'I was stunned,' he told me, 'I could not believe how they had found out about my visit to Amritsar. My family absolutely refused to let me go again. It was my last visit. I simply dropped the contract.' The infiltration by the extremists into public services and institutions extended to the police, the civil administration, educational institutions and communications. The network was so extensive that almost any kind of information required was immediately available. 'Even their telephone calls from the Golden Temple had priority at the exchange when we first arrived,' an army general told me after the Operation.

Although it is clear that it was through this network that Bhindranwale and his men acquired weapons, it is easier to establish that the large sums of money extorted from local traders, businessmen and industrialists was funnelled into purchase of arms. And it was not only members of the rank and file of the militant leadership who were assigned the task of collecting funds. In the organized and controlled heirarchy that Bhindranwale and his chief lieutenant Amreek Singh of the All India Sikh Students Federation headed, they set the example. The following is a first person account given to me by a well-known jeweller in Amritsar's Guru Bazaar of his direct encounter with Bhindranwale and Amreek Singh. The account is reliable if only because the jeweller, a man in his mid-sixties, is a reputable figure whose family has operated their business in the city for over a hundred years and also because the man's style is so low-key and cool-headed that his story is unlikely to appear exaggerated.

'Some time in the second week of March this year,' says the jeweller, 'I received a telephone call at my residence from Bhai Amreek Singh of the AISSF. I had never met the man before, only heard of him. After introducing himself, he politely asked me if I could spare a little time that evening. He said that Sant Bhindranwale wished to see me, and could I make myself available for his darshan on the rooftop of the Langar building. I could not inquire what the reason was because the call was disconnected. But as you can imagine I was exceedingly worried. For months one had heard all kinds of stories, and I even knew certain families that had suffered, but as far as I knew, no other jeweller had been sent for.

'I spent a very nervous day and, at a little before five in the evening, made my way to the Langar. I gave my name to the armed men at the entrance and after a few minutes, Bhai Amreek Singh himself appeared and escorted me inside. He motioned me to sit down with the sangat (congregation) who were listening to Bhindranwale speaking. I had never seen the sant before.

'After about an hour, the sant ended his talk and rose to leave himself. Most of the people also rose to go. It was then that Bhai Amreek Singh, having whispered a few words to the sant, took me up to meet him personally. He smiled and said that he was honoured that Amritsar's most famous jeweller had come to visit him. I simply stood there with folded hands. Then he asked me, without much fuss and within earshot of people standing around him, that since my family and I were such old devotees of Darbar Sahib, didn't I think that we should make a donation.

'I stood there completely silent. Quickly he said, "How about twenty kilos of gold? Does that suit you?" and began moving towards the door. I could not believe his request. It was as if the ground was slipping from beneath my feet, I was so shaky. I fell down at his feet and pleaded. I will be ruined, I said, I do not have that kind of money. I am not a bullion merchant, I am only a man who works with other people's gold. I will have to sell out to make that kind of contribution.

'He was not a bit irritated. In fact, he started laughing. "All you rich men are the same", he said, and added that I could if liked, pay the sum in monthly instalments. But I kept clutching to his feet and saying that even a kilo of gold a month was too much, have some mercy on me and my family. "Okay, okay," he said, half a kilo then, but remember every month we should get it and there should be no lapses.'

'It was downright extortion and it took place openly. There was nothing I could do about it and for the first month, till the payment was made in the form of gold ornaments, I did not tell a soul including members of my family. But I began to fear for my sons and my grandchildren. The whole matter weighed so heavily on me, that it worsened my heart condition. I was bitter, disgusted. Sometimes it seemed to me that it was worth closing down the business in Amritsar and moving to another city. In fact, I sent one of my sons away to investigate opening a shop in Delhi. But we count ourselves lucky. In the end, we paid out about two lakh rupees. But you can imagine our relief when the army moved in and ended the menace of the sant. Having gone through such an experience, tell me, do you blame me for feeling relief that the Bhindranwale hurricane that threatened to wipe us out has ended?'

It was not only Hindu traders who were coerced to making such donations – Sikhs too, except perhaps they were not pressurized as strongly. 'Bhindranwale was secular in one thing-he spared no one, Hindu or Sikh, in making money,' says Sardar Dilbir Singh, a member of the executive of the Chief Khalsa Diwan, an important Sikh charitable trust, in Amritsar. But there are enough instances to prove that some Hindus, especially if they were perceived as leaders of public opinion, came in for a harsher sentence. The best-known, and widely documented, example is the family of Lala Jagat Narain in Jullundur, owners of the Hind Samachar group of newspapers.

In August 1983, the last occasion I met Ramesh Chander, Lala Jagat Narain's son, he was already a man under great stress. Carrying on valiantly as editor of the paper, his daily mail included at least a couple of abusive, threatening letters. Anonymous callers made it impossible for him to pick up his telephone directly. Two gunmen and two bodyguards stood at the bottom of the stairs leading to his office; later a personal bodyguard travelled with him everywhere. After his father's murder, Chander seemed to be under continuous attack from the Sikh leadership. When his paper published a calendar with a picture of Guru Gobind Singh, with a small picture of his late father in the margin, the SGPC claimed that it 'injured the feelings of Sikhs' and demanded an apology. Bhindranwale called it an insult, and declared that any Sikh who took revenge on Chander for such a sacrilege would be honoured. 'I am bitter,' Chander had then said, 'but not against Sikhs, only against certain sections of the Sikh leadership. Of course, one has become cautious, cautious even in attending public functions.'

That caution proved ineffective as, stepping out of a function in the city's public library on 12 May 1984, the spirit of revenge overpowered him. As he drove past a crowded roundabout in broad daylight Chander was gunned down by a group of Sikhs passing by in a speeding car. His gunman was seated behind and could do nothing. Nor could a police patrol on duty; they simply disappeared when the cold-blooded murder was brought to their notice. Chander's body lay at the spot for several hours and even the district commissioner, with whom he had left the function, could exercise no immediate decision to have it taken away or control the angry mob that collected.

Chander's two sons, twenty-eight-year-old Ashwini Minna and twenty-two-year-old Arvind now occupy bis office. They carry revolvers and have not stepped out of the office since the day of their father's death. Each day the mail brings more threatening letters, and the boys continue to fear for their life even after the army action. There are now pickets with soldiers on duty round the clock at the bottom of the stairs and the roof of the building is equipped with a wireless, morchas, searchlights and a whole platoon of CRP men. When Minna crosses the street to his house, he is escorted by four guards armed with Sten guns. 'I was counting my days after my father's death,' he says, 'and even now the threat has not gone. Communal feelings have grown since the Operation. And, frankly, if the army is not posted in Punjab for another six months to a year, there could be thousand Bhindranwales sprouting everywhere.'

Virendra, owner and editor of the Vir Pratap group of newspapers, and his son Chander Mohan, echo Minna's sentiments. They see a continued army presence as a prerequisite to long-term peace in Punjab. 'It's necessary at a time when communal passions are aroused,' says Chander Mohan. Like other forthright members of Punjab's Hindu elite, Chander and his father consider themselves secular, but say that their championing of Hindu pressure groups such as Punjabi Hindu Sangathan in Jullundur, the Rashtriya Suraksha Samiti in Amritsar and the Hindu Suraksha Samiti in Patiala, was forced upon them as a measure of self-defence. Their attempts to bring these organizations together, however, has proved feeble, given lack of popular support and a unified leadership. But they feel that the effort must be kept up if only to check further escalation of communal tension.

One reason why the advent of communal emotion is centred in the town of Punjab is because over 80 per cent of its non-Sikh population is concentrated in urban areas. Its effect in rural society is marginal, there being no more than a handful of Hindus each in Punjab's 12,000 villages. Where they exist, usually in the role of the local *bania* (trader) or *artiya* (commission agent), they are so well-knit into the social fabric that the Sikhs tend to be protective of them in a time of crisis.

That, however, does not imply that Punjab's rural areas are devoid of tension or have remained unaffected by the army's action or its presence. Its villages are as convulsed by a wave of anger as its cities, only the emphasis of the reaction is different and the resentment directed at other targets. In the villages the army is seen as the chief aggressor in its phase of flushing out the countryside of extremists and rounding up of weapons. On the other hand, Bhindranwale's image has rocketed into the realm of the supernatural. Here and there some villagers may express dissent, or doubt the general impression, but by and large Bhindranwale and his defence of the Akal Takht has become part of everyday folklore. And Punjab's gurdwara towns, particularly those where the army was engaged in fighting extremists, thwarted religious fervour has resulted in an atmosphere of sullen gloom. Preposterous stories abound. 'In his (Bhindranwale's) village in district Faridkot,' says a shopkeeper outside the gurdwara in Tarn Taran doing brisk business in the sale of *kirpans* and the black bands to which they were attached, 'his family have special *amrit* kept in a glass bottle. So far its colour is clear which means Sant Jarnail Singh is alive. He left it at home before returning to the Darbar Sahib to take on the Indian army, and said that no one was to fear for his life, till the colour of the liquid turned red. Someone who came back from his village told me that it has not. His family is confident that he is safe and well somewhere.'

In Bhindranwale's own gurdwara at Chowk Mehta about 40 kilometres outside Amritsar, the gloom is all pervasive. The gurdwara is empty save for a few villagers including a plumber and an eccentric-looking, stooping character called Sukha Singh who has bicycled for two days from a village a hundred kilometres away to check things out at Chowk Mehta. 'My friends and family in the village warned me: Don't go, they said, the army will definitely get you. But I said to them, 'Let the army get me. What is a Sikh worth these days, any way? I must go and find out what happened to the sant.' Understanding nods of approval from everyone in the mourning group, including the vocal plumber Ajit Singh, who says: 'Would you have believed such a day would come? That the army would attack our gurdwaras and us. They've broken our .backs. Brother, you are from the city, and you should go back and write that in Punjab every man who wears a turban and keeps a beard is called a terrorist. They have dragged men from their homes here and flogged them and kept them in jail without any explanation. They have taken our cash offerings from our gurdwaras and ransacked our stores. The very same army that was proud of its Sikh soldiers has begun to commit atrocities upon them.'

About 70 kilometres southwest of Moga town in district Faridkot is Bhindranwale's hometown of Roda. He was born here, his family lives here and the entire community seems to bask in the reflected glory of its somewhat sinister connection. Past large village houses splashed with 'Join AISSF' slogans, we arrive at an airy house built around a traditional open courtyard. It is easily recognizable as Bhindranwale's family home because of cars parked outside. They belong not to his family but to prosperous visitors from Faridkot and Moga who are visiting the late Sant's birthplace. As a centre of pilgrimage, Roda is fast gaining importance since the death of its most famous son. And as the chief perpetuator of the Bhindranwale myth, his father Jathedar Joginder Singh, a man in his late seventies with a long white beard and bushy, furrowing eyebrows, proves to be the centre of attraction.

He is holding court to a group of villagers and two prosperous-looking young couples who have arrived in the cars. This is educated small town gentry: the women speak English in convent school accent and their husbands argue vehemently with a religious zeal difficult to reconcile with urban education.

After a few minutes of listening to Bhindranwale's father, it is easy to spot the similarities with his son. He speaks with the same irrational rhetoric and rabble-rousing passion that leaves no room for lucid argument or open-ended dialogue. It is difficult to carry on a conversation. Too many questions are fielded with a mixture of shrill contempt and shrewd evasion. He is convinced that his son was possessed of super human prowess, physical and spiritual, from the day of his birth – rather is, because he firmly believes that Jarnail Singh is not dead, and snaps angrily at people who use the past tense. He remembers that Jarnail Singh, as a young boy, was an all-round prodigy; 'someone,' in his words, 'who could fell a tree in a single blow and at the same time memorize whole chapters of the Granth and recite them a hundred times a day,' It is improbable that the old man's memory serves him right; in fact he hardly knew his son and, in recent years, used to visit him at the Golden Temple like any ordinary devotee. Bhindranwale left his village when he was an adolescent to join the itinerant band of religious preachers headed by Sant Gurcharan Singh Bhindranwale from whom he later inherited the mantle of the Bhindranwale seat in Chowk Mehta. Jarnail Singh rarely returned home after that, though he was later married. His wife and two young sons continue to live in the same house in Roda but are kept strictly in purdah, especially when the press is visiting.

'He was only a preacher of religion,' the father is saying of Jarnail Singh, 'one of the greatest the Sikh faith has ever produced. What did he ask of the Sikhs but that they should read *gurbani*, keep their beards untrimmed, take *amrit* and leave liquor. Was that too much from a man who all his life stuck to all spiritual disciplines? Was it too much for the government who called him a terrorist, a rebel, a hater of Hindus and accused him of murders and dacoities.'

The monologue was unceasing. But I had not bargained for the electrifying effect the old man's words would have on the affluent visitors from Moga and Faridkot. Turning around to one of the men, I casually asked what he thought was the general Sikh reaction to the army operation. There was a pause before I realized that the man was choking with sobs. Tears were pouring down his face. He was shaking with a grief so private and sudden that his words were a barely-audible sputter: 'You don't and can't understand,' he said bitterly, 'what Sikhs feel like. We are helpless. We cannot react. We have become incapable of reaction.'

His wife sitting on the other side of the old man's cot was brushing away her own tears. 'I'll tell you,' she said, 'what it feels like. It feels as if you have been stripped naked and assaulted. Religion, after all, is a very private thing. And a place of worship has a special privacy, call it mystique. That has gone because it has been brutally invaded. The sanctity of our gurdwaras is gone forever. How can the government ever compensate that?'

As I left the old man began to rail once again: 'I can tell you that only God knows what the consequence of this diabolical action will be. The rule of those who have attacked the Darbar Sahib will end as fatefully as the rule of Turks and Mughals who attacked it in the past. It is God's home and God has his own way of taking revenge.'

Such scenes of pent-up anguish verging on hysteria were common place in the villages of Punjab in the aftermath of Operation Bluestar. Its effects were so various and wide-ranging that it was difficult to arrive at precise conclusions and construct a credible hypothesis. One could only sense that, like a deep-rooted tree struck by some massive bolt of lightning, there were cracks and fissures that spread in every direction along the central communal split. But if one were to isolate the causes of resentment and pain of the aggrieved community as a whole, if one stripped the layers of local and personal factors to listen, as it were, the changed cadence of people's inner voices and record the irreparable damage inflicted on their beliefs, two major factors emerged as contributory to the post-Bluestar crisis.

One was the total lack of speedy and accurate information about what exactly happened during the Operation and what was the extent of damage to the Golden Temple. The importance of this factor cannot be emphasized enough, in view of the fact that government media erred dangerously. All India Radio's white-washed news bulletins and Doordarshan's mindlessly repeatist visual imagery were designed to deceive, as if the information had to be doctored for the benefit of an enemy. This succeeded in intensifying the trauma, especially in the villages where accurate information disseminated at regular intervals is hard to obtain at the best of times. Villagers, if and where possible, plugged into foreign networks for whatever scraps of information they could obtain. The BBC became the norm, and Radio Pakistan came a close second. Even to the uneducated peasant, unaware of the intricacies of the long-drawn-out negotiations between the Akalis and the government and their subsequent breakdown, it appeared excessive to have to listen six times a day news of protestors marching daily to the gates of the British High Commission to register their grievance over the BBC's broadcast of an interview with self-styled Khalistan leader Jagjit Singh Chauhan eight thousand miles away. Certainly, the incessant drum-beating of didactic lessons in Hindu-Sikh harmony must have sounded callous when in fact they were at their lowest ebb. And for those with access to television, opinion clips (repeated insensitively, as many as three times an evening) of certain Sikhs lauding the army action at a moment when the Sikh reaction was one of unequivocal horror no doubt drove large sections of viewers to switch off their sets. In the circumstances, it was rumour that took over: word-of-mouth stories, mixed fabrication and fact and swept Punjab's villages for as long as three weeks after the army action.

The other factor that continues to prolong the after-effects of the trauma is the continuing presence of the army. It is not in the scope of this chapter to discuss what its effects in national terms may be, or what, in fact, is the effect upon the army itself, but in Punjab's rural society the antagonism against the army is steadily grown. This is due to its role of flushing the countryside of extremists and weapons, a role made more complicated by the villagers' perception of the armed force as an aggressor, not an impartial arbiter involved in restoring law and order. Such a devaluation was inevitable but possible to redress if the army's stay or its authority was limited. As it is not, the devaluation grows proportionately in the public mind. And while it is true that certain sections of Punjab's population, especially urban Hindus, argue vociferously that its presence is a necessity, their insecurity only betrays the government's bleak disinterest in either finding a political solution or applying the healing touch. No such touch is possible in Punjab so long as towns and villages are treated as border outposts, and kept under surveillance by soldiers and bayonets.

The combination of these two factors – delayed information and an extensive army presence – is exemplified by what happened in a small village, six kilometres outside Moga town. On the morning of 7 June, as Operation Bluestar was in full swing inside the Golden Temple, the village of Talwandi Bagherian became tangled in an unexpected encounter with the army. The army version is that as some troops on a routine patrol approached the village, about 12 rounds were fired from within. A jawan was seriously injured and another wounded.

Two weeks after the incident, the village was still in a state of nervous shock, brought upon partly by shock and partly by mourning. The sarpanch, together with about a dozen others, was still under interrogation, but the village cooperative's secretary, took us to meet members of the panchayat. These turned out to be two elderly men. They led us first to the house of Jagan Singh, a young inhabitant who had been killed as a result of the confrontation.

Then, in the courtyard of the village gurdwara – a ramshackle building in the shade of a neem tree – the villagers congregated to give their version of the incident. Amidst the rising cacophony of voices and arguments, they failed to answer the basic question: what led them to fire unprovoked upon the soldiers?

One of the panchayat members, Pooran Singh, silenced all the others to answer on behalf of the village. 'I will tell you the truth,' he said. 'Yes, it is true that the villagers fired first, the sarpanch and Jagan Singh who the army took away and then later brought back dead. But the reality is that these men fired at the approaching soldiers out of confusion. We have no terrorists here, tell me do any of us look like terrorists? For a few days before 7 June we had been hearing stories of what happened in Amritsar. Then we heard that the Darbar Sahib was in shambles. And every main gurdwara in Punjab was under attack by the army. The local boys became very agitated. When we saw the army coming, we thought they had come to take our gurdwara. It was just that and nothing else. Sikhs will see their homes burn, but not their guru's home.'

In the simple words of a peasant, Pooran Singh had truthfully summed up the feelings of his village. True, lack of information about the army action in the Golden Temple, was one reason for the inhabitants of a small village to mobilize themselves into unprovoked action. In a Punjab fallen silent under the rule of the army, it was understandable that a group of isolated villagers suddenly saw themselves as autonomous defenders of their faith. But the underlining emotion that led them into action was not their religious fervour; it was fear. Fear of one kind and another has become the keynote of the crisis in Punjab.

At first, it was fear of the terrorists. Then it was fear of the army. Now it is fear by one community facing reprisals from another if the army vacates the state. And the largest fear of all, bred by a mistrust of the government and its actions. It is these multiple and growing fears that have made the people of Punjab become partisan, in a defensive, demeaning way. It has transformed, in a matter of a couple of years, a dynamic, integrated, prosperous society into a fragmented, militant and embittered one. While the government jockeys for new stratagems to retain its position of strength, and prolongs its search for the healing touch to repair the communal chasm and defuse tensions, the future of Punjab defies political solution.

The model state, the flourishing frontier state, the great granary of India and the communally trouble-free state has now become a national problem. Repairing the Akal Takht under army control will not repair the greater divide created in Punjab. Allowing the army to linger will only breed a more invidious form of Sikh extremism in the future. The answer is to purge the state of fear. That can only be achieved not by demanding assurances from one community or one section of the people but by giving assurances. Or else Punjab's continuing drift towards the dangerous extremities of social disintegration, economic despair and communal alienation will bring it back to the brink again.

White Paper on Punjab Agitation: A Summary

ISSUED BY THE GOVERNMENT OF INDIA

I. INTRODUCTION

During the last three years Punjab has been the scene of a series of agitations. Four distinct factors were noticeably at work:

The agitations sponsored by the Shiromani Akali Dal;

A stridently communal and extremist movement which degenerated into open advocacy of violence and sanction for the most heinous crimes against innocent and helpless citizens and against the state;

Secessionist and anti-national activities; and

Involvement of criminals, smugglers, other anti-social elements and Naxalites who took advantage of the situation for their own ends.

The secessionist agitations and terrorist groups took advantage of the cover of agitations provided by the Akali Dal leadership to pursue a systematic plan of stockpiling of arms and ammunition in places of worship and of misusing the sacred precincts of the Golden Temple and other gurdwaras to direct and commit acts of murder, sabotage, arson and loot. Simultaneoulsy, a determined effort was made to drive a wedge between Hindus and Sikhs.

Gradually a secessionist and anti-national movement, with the active support of a small number of groups operating from abroad, dominated the scene. The Akali Dal leadership surrendered the initiative and control over the agitation to the terrorists and was unwilling to negotiate a settlement on the basis of any reasonable framework offered by the government.

The government made every possible effort to bring about a settlement. Till the very last moment discussions were held with the Akali Dal leaders who were found to be more rigid than before.

The subversive activities of terrorists had assumed menacing proportions in the context of India's security environment. The influence of external forces, with deep-rooted interests in the disintegration of India, was becoming evident. In these circumstances the army was called in to meet the challenge to the security, unity and integrity of the country.

II
DEMANDS OF THE SHIROMANI AKALI DAL AND GOVERNMENT RESPONSE

The Akali Dal sponsored an agitation in support of a set of demands submitted to the government in October 1981. Some of these demands had their origin in a resolution, generally known as the Anandpur Sahib Resolution, adopted by the Akali Dal in October 1973. The resolution asked for the immediate merger with Punjab of Punjabi-speaking Sikh-populated areas in Haryana, Rajasthan and Himachal Pradesh besides

Chandigarh. It also sought a fundamental change in the centre-state relations, restricting the role of the centre to defence, foreign affairs, post and telecommunications, currency and railways. The authenticated version of the resolution, issued in November 1982, emphasized the constitution of 'a single administrative unit where the interests of Sikhs and Sikhism are specially protected.'

The prime minister met the representatives of the Akali Dal on 16 October 1981 and thereafter again on two occasions in November 1981 and April 1982. The process of consultation and discussion initiated thus has not been interrupted by the government since then. There have been several rounds of talks, both open and secret, as well as tripartite discussions in which leaders of opposition parties in parliament also participated. Annexure IV of the White Paper documents, the large number of meetings held with the representatives of the Akali Dal.

The main issues discussed with the Akali Dal representatives fall into three broad categories, viz.,

(i) those which concern the Sikh community as a religious group;
(ii) those which relate to other states besides Punjab; and
(iii) general issues.

(i) Demands which Concern the Sikh Community as a Religious Group

The religious demands finally put forward by the Akali Dal were:

(a) Grant of 'holy city' status to Amritsar on the pattern of Hardwar, Kashi and Kurukshetra;
(b) Installation of 'Harmandir Radio' at the Golden Temple to relay *kirtan*;
(c) Permission to Sikhs travelling by air to wear *kirpans* on domestic and international flights; and
(d) Enactment of All India Gurdwara Act.

(a) Grant of 'Holy City' Status to Amritsar

The government has not conferred 'holy city' status on the cities mentioned or any other city. Restrictions on the sale of meat or liquor in cities like Hardwar and Kurukshetra had been imposed by the local authorities or state governments. On 27 February 1983 the prime minister announced that the sale of tobacco, liquor and meat would be banned in a demarcated area around the Golden Temple as well as the Durgiana temple in Amritsar. Action has already been taken in pursuance of this announcement and shops selling tobacco, liquor and meat within a radius of 200 metres of Harmandir Sahib and Durgiana temple have already been shifted. The grant of 'holy city' status as such to any city is not in consonance with the secular nature of our Constitution.

(b) Installation of Transmitter Station at the Golden Temple

While private radio broadcasting facilities cannot be allowed to any group, the government offered to arrange for direct relay of shabad kirtan from the Golden Temple through the Jalundur station of All India Radio. However, the Shiromani Gurdwara Parbandhak Committee did not extend the requisite facilities to the All India Radio authorities.

(c) Carrying *Kirpans* on Flights

Instructions were issued in February 1983 permitting Sikh passengers to carry *kirpans* which do not exceed 22.8 cm (9 inch) in length and whose blade length does not exceed 15.24 cm (6 inch) on domestic flights. International regulations do not permit carrying of weapons on international carriers.

(d) All India Gurdwara Act

On 27 February 1983 the prime minister announced that governments of the states where the gurdwaras are located and the managements of the gurdwaras would be consulted to arrive at the consensus needed for enacting such a legislation.

(ii) Disputes which Relate to Other States besides Punjab

(a) River Waters

The government was agreeable to rescinding the agreement of 31 December 1981 between the governments of Punjab, Haryana and Rajasthan and to refer the dispute regarding the surplus waters of Ravi-Beas to a tribunal presided over by a judge of the Supreme Court under the Inter-state Water Disputes Act, 1956 to determine afresh the allocation between the two states. However, the Akali Dal wanted to reopen the 1955 agreement on the basis of which arid and dry lands of the Indus basin in Rajasthan are being irrigated. It also wanted the Yamuna waters to be taken into account. The widening of the scope of the dispute relating to the Ravi-Beas waters was obviously not acceptable to Haryana and Rajasthan as well as to the central government.

The prime minister had assured the Akali Dal that the interests of Punjab would not be affected. She suggested that a committee of experts should go into the whole question of augmenting the availability of water in the basin. Its recommendations would receive priority consideration by government. Even these assurances had no effect in changing the rigid position of the Akali Dal.

(b) Territorial Issue

In 1966 the Shah Commission recommended that Chandigarh be given to Haryana. However, in 1970 Smt Indira Gandhi, as prime minister, announced that Chandigarh would go to Punjab. Under this decision:

(1) The capital project area of Chandigarh would go to Punjab;
(2) A part of Fazilka Tehsil (including Abohar) of Ferozepur district of Punjab would be transferred to Haryana; and
(3) As regards other claims and counter-claims for the readjustment of inter-state boundaries, a commission would be appointed.

The above decision could not be implemented due to the change in the attitude of the state.

The government has indicated their willingness to abide by any one of the following alternatives:

(1) Implementation of the 1970 decision;
(2) Referring all disputes and claims including Chandigarh to a new commission;
(3) Dividing Chandigarh between Punjab and Haryana, with Punjab getting the major share, and referring the remaining disputes to a commission; or
(4) Adopting any other alternative acceptable to both states.

Within the above framework a large number of different formulations were proposed, none of which was acceptable to the Akali Dal leadership.

The prime minister has repeatedly declared that Chandigarh would go to Punjab provided Haryana were suitably compensated. As late as on 2 June 1984, the prime minister in her broadcast reiterated that Chandigarh would go to Punjab provided Haryana gets its share of some Hindi-speaking areas which are now in Punjab.

The Akali Dal is, however, adamant that Chandigarh should be transferred to Punjab immediately and other disputes referred to a Commission. Thus the stalemate continues.

(iii) General Issues

(a) Centre-state Relations

Government set up in June 1983 a Commission under Chairman Justice Ranjit Singh Sarkaria to examine and review the existing arrangements between the union and the states in regard to powers, function and responsibilities in all spheres and recommended such changes or measures as may be appropriate. The commission was to keep in view the scheme and the framework of the constitution designed to ensure the unity and integrity of the country. The government invited the Akali Dal to make any submissions it wished before the Sarkaria Commission within its terms of reference. However, the Akali Dal insisted that the government make a specific mention of the Anandpur Sahib Resolution, which restricts the central role of foreign affairs, defence, currency and communications, while referring the matter to the Sarkaria Commission.

During the discussions, the Akali Dal had agreed not to press this. But subsequently Sant Harchand Singh Longowal, president of the Akali Dal, reiterated the demand.

The Anandpur Sahib Resolution is at total variance with the basic concept of the unity and integrity of the nation as expressed in our constitution. It cannot be accepted as a basis for discussion.

(b) Other Demands

Among their other demands, the Akali Dal representatives emphasized the following two as issues of special concern to them:

(i) Grant of second language status to Punjabi language in Haryana, Delhi, Himachal Pradesh and Rajasthan.
(ii) Stopping the uprooting of Punjabi farmers from Terai areas of Uttar Pradesh.

(i) Second Language Status for Punjabi Language: The demand for the teaching of Punjabi as a second language in areas of Haryana and Rajasthan, where there is a sizable

Punjabi-speaking population, can be met within the framework of the three language formula agreed at the chief ministers' Conference in 1961. This was explained to the Akali Dal. Delhi, Haryana, Rajasthan and Himachal Pradesh have taken action to provide facilities to teach Punjabi at the primary and the secondary stages.

(ii) Punjabi Farmers in the Terai Region of U.P.: The state government of Uttar Pradesh have denied that Sikh farmers were being uprooted from the terai area. The state legislation is intended to prevent unauthorized occupation of tribal land. The Tharu and Buxar tribes have been dispossessed of substantial areas of land cultivated by them prior to 1947. Of the 7860 unauthorized occupants, more than 5000 were from Uttar Pradesh itself, and one common policy was being followed with regard to all such persons. Local authorities had been directed to take action only in accordance with the principles of natural justice and within the framework of the law.

(c) Amendment of Article 25(2)(b) of the Constitution

A completely new demand was raised by the Akali Dal in January 1984 asking for an amendment of Article 25(2)(b) of the Constitution. Simultaneously, an agitation was announced for burning and mutilation of copies of the Constitution of India. Even though this demand was raised, the Akali Dal was not clear about the nature of the amendment. On 1 May 1984, it was reported that the SGPC president had constituted a 21-member committee of experts to suggest relevant amendments.

Even though the government maintains that Article 25(2)(b), far from weakening the distinct identity of the Sikh community, was in fact a recognition of that identity, it wanted to allay any misgiving on this point. Accordingly the home minister declared on 31 March 1984 that the government would be prepared to consult the SGPC and other representatives of the Sikh community as well as legal experts and undertake such legislation by way of amendment as may be necessary to remove such doubts.

The Akali Dal also wanted to link the demands for the amendment of Article 25 with the idea of a separate personal law for the Sikhs. However, no concrete proposals have been submitted.

The timing and manner in which the demand for amendment of Article 25 was presented are typical of the Akali Dal's approach to negotiations. When some issues appeared to have been settled, new issues were raised, thereby frustrating the possibility of a settlement. The Akali Dal appeared to want to keep an agitation going on some issue or other, regardless of the consequences of such agitation which progressively grew more and more violent.

III
TERROR AND VIOLENCE IN PUNJAB

The sectarian feud between some fundamentalist Sikhs and Nirankaris was the starting point of the tragic events in Punjab. The clashes of April 1978 and later were climaxed by the assassination of Baba Gurbachan Singh, the spiritual head of the Nirankaris, on 24 April 1980. Thereafter, dogmatism and extremism, accompanied by terror and violence, were to overwhlem the political life of Punjab.

Structure of Voilence

In the course of time communal separatism became an integral part of a movement which was started in the name of grievances of all Punjabis. This outcome was dictated by the interaction of the forces at work. The agitation of the Akali Dal, the virulent communalism bred by extremism and the secessionist and anti-national activities of a small group, largely supported by external elements, formed a symbiotic relationship. Added to this was the combination of several disparate groups and individuals such as smugglers, other criminals and Naxalites who took advantage of the unsettled conditions. Many who thought that the political aspect could be isolated from the problems of terrorism and secessionism overlooked the complex and changing pattern of these relationships. However, the politics of extremist violence have their own dynamics. It is only a matter of time before they subjugate other tendencies. This has happened before, and it is not surprising that in Punjab also violence and terror gained the upper hand.

The Akali Dal did not unequivocally condemn the killings, arson and loot which were enveloping the state. Nor did it denounce the poisonous propaganda of communal fanatics. Similarly, the misuse of the Golden Temple and other shrines for accumulation of large quantities of arms and ammunition, for providing shelter to murderers and criminals and for making detailed preparations for subversion and insurgency, drew no protest from the Akali Dal leadership who even denied the very existence of such activities. An aggressive group, operating from within the Golden Temple complex, gradually enlarged the scale of violence, in full confidence that the political leadership would not call it to account.

Even before the Akali Dal submitted its demands to the government, the All India Sikh Students Federation and the Dal Khalsa began to incite communal passions. The arrest of Shri Bhindranwale on 20 September 1981 in connection with the murder of Lala Jagat Narain earlier in the month sparked off large-scale violence in Mehta Chowk where the police were attacked with deadly weapons. The same day motorcycle riders killed four persons in Jullundur, starting the cult of killings by motorcyclists. On 29 September 1981 an Indian Airlines plane was hijacked to Lahore by some Sikh extremists.

The Growth of Militancy

This was the background for the start of the Akali agitation in April-May 1982. On 19 July 1982 Shri Amreek Singh, president, All India Sikh Students Federation (AISSF), was arrested in connection with a case of an attempted murder. The same day Shri Bhindranwale shifted his headquarters from Chowk Mehta to Guru Nank Niwas within the Golden Temple complex, a move which had significant implications for future developments.

On 4 August 1982 the Akali Dal intensified its *morcha* describing it as a 'Dharam Yudh.' Two incidents of hijacking of Indian Airlines planes followed. Shri Bhindranwale and others in the Golden Temple complex began to extol and instigate violence.

The government released all arrested Akali Dal agitators in October 1982 to facilitate talks, and repeatedly appealed to the Akali Dal leadership to give up the path of confrontation. The response of the Akali Dal consisted of announcements of a series of agitations from November 1982 to June 1983, including the threat of demonstrations during the Asian Games, in November-December 1982. Throughout this period conscientious police officers were systematically done to death, the gravest of all such crimes being the dastardly murder of Shri A.S. Atwal, deputy inspector general, Jalundur Range, on 25 April 1983 just as he was coming out of the Darbar Sahib after prayers. The AISSF started from June 1983 onwards to use Gurmat camps to propagate extremism and communal ideology and to impart training in arms.

The Communal Dimension

A new dimension to the escalating violence in Punjab was now given with the deliberate move to kill members of the Hindu community. On 5 October 1983 a bus was hijacked near Dhilwan in Kapurthala district and six Hindu passengers were murdered after being segregated from other passengers. On 18

November 1983 another four Hindu passengers travelling in a bus in Amritsar district were similarly killed.

The situation had acquired dimensions which had wider implications for the security and the unity and integrity of the country. Recognizing this the chief minister of Punjab resigned and the state was brought under president's rule with effect from 6 October 1983. Several legislative and administrative measures were taken to curb terrorists.

Misuse of the Akal Takht

On 15 December 1983 Shri Bhindranwale moved from the Guru Nanak Niwas to the Akal Takht with his armed entourage. From this sanctuary he and his associates intensified incitements of violence and communal hatred. An important target of extremists were those Sikhs who opposed their anti-national activities. They were liquidated in a planned manner. A similar fate befell those within the Golden Temple complex who were judged to have defied the authority of the extremists. Several were tortured and subjected to painful death, their bodies then being thrown into open drains. Desecration of the Golden Temple complex extended to other, equally reprehensible, form.

Unmindful of the surcharged atmosphere in the state the Akali Dal announced on 26 January 1984 a new agitation for burning Article 25 of the Constitution of India. A Punjab *bandh* was called on 8 February 1984, which was followed by a *bandh* on 14 February 1984 called by the Hindu Suraksha Samiti. Serious clashes and violence resulted in the death of 11 persons. Some Hindu fanatics committed the sacrilege of damaging the model of the Golden Temple and a picture of Guru Ram Dass at the Amritsar Railway Station.

The extremists now felt bold enough to engage the security forces. The people lived in constant fear and were unwilling to give any information about the criminal activities of terrorists. Several tenants and house owners in the proximity of the Golden Temple were forcibly evicted from their dwellings.

The February 1984 Negotiations

The government made yet another effort to break the stalemate in Punjab. A tripartite meeting was convened on 14 February 1984. A new wave of violence in Punjab followed. There was violence in Haryana also. More innocent lives were lost including those of eight Sikhs in Panipat on 19 February 1984. The Akali Dal refused to continue the negotiations at the tripartite meeting which had adjourned on 15 February 1984 to meet again within a few days. The pattern of violence now clearly bore the impression of a well thought-out plan to plunge Punjab into anarchy. People were killed at random. Nine were shot dead on 21 February 1984, eleven on 23 February and fifteen on 24 February and again 3 on 24 February. Shri H.S. Manchanda, president of the Delhi Gurdwara Parbandhak Committee, was shot dead in Delhi on 28 March 1984 and Dr V.N. Tewari, MP, a professor at the Panjab University, on 3 April 1984 in Chandigarh.

Antisocial and other criminal elements indulged in the looting of banks and business establishments. Over the period from 1 October 1983 to 31 May 1984, twenty-four banks were robbed. Large amounts of cash were looted and guards and other personnel killed.

The Killings of April-May 1984

The violent incidents in April-May 1984 bring out clearly the real character and designs of the terrorists. The AISSF indulged in widespread acts of arson to prevent the holding of examinations. A college principal in Ferozepur was shot dead on 1 April 1984. Murders of prominent politicians, religious leaders and journalists followed. On 11 May 1984, a *kar seva* truck belonging to the Mehta Chowk gurdwara was apprehended and Sten guns, arms and ammunition recovered.

Shri Bhindranwale sent out instructions that in the event of any government action, terrorists in the rural areas were to kill Hindus and central government employees and to move in large numbers to the temple. On some days as many as a dozen killings were reported. Although the Sikh masses broadly remained unaffected by these developments, it was obvious that a situation of insurgency in open defiance of constituted authority was building up.

Akali Dal's Call for a New Agitation from 3 June

Even at this late hour the Akali Dal could have drawn back from the precipice of anarchy. But it chose to call for another agitation starting 3 June. The government started a fresh round of negotiations in May 1984 but unfortunately due to the hardening of the Akali Dal's position no settlement could be reached. Even the last minute appeal by the prime minister in a nation-wide broadcast on 2 June 1984 was spurned.

From 4 August 1982, when the Akali Morcha was started up to 3 June 1984, there were over 1200 violent incidents in which 410 persons were killed and more than 1180 injured. From 1 January 1984 to 3 June 1984, there were over 775 violent incidents in which 298 persons were killed and more than 525 injured.

Parliament's Concern

Throughout this period the parliament continued to express its concern at the deteriorating situation in Punjab and affirmed the national resolve to meet the menace of terrorism, extremism and communalism.

Separatism Based Abroad

Several secessionist Sikh organizations are operating abroad. The chief among them which have raised the slogan of 'Khalistan' or a 'separate Sikh State' are the National Council of Khalistan, Dal Khalsa, Babbar Khalsa and Akhand Kirtani Jatha.

The National Council of Khalistan headed by Dr Jagjit Singh Chauhan is active in UK, West Germany, Canada and USA. The Dal Khalsa activities are mainly in UK and West Germany, while the Babbar Khalsa operat largely from Vancouver in Canada. The Akhand Kirtani Jatha has units in UK and Canada.

Dr Jagjit Singh Chauhan, the self-styled leader of the so-called Khalistan movement has been trying to whip up anti-India feelings abroad. He has been organizing demonstrations, burning the Indian national flag and making provocative statements. On 26 January 1984 the secretary general of the National Council of Khalistan, Shri Balbir Singh Sandhu, hoisted what he described as the Khalistan flag on one of the buildings near Harmandir Sahib. Dr Chauhan has been lobbying with leaders in foreign countries, particularly in the United States of America. He has also established contacts with leaders of the Jammu & Kashmir Liberation Front in UK. He has resorted to gimmicks such as the issue of the Khalistan passport, postage stamps and currency notes.

The Dal Khalsa advocates use of violence to achieve its objective of an independent sovereign Sikh state. It claimed responsibility for hijacking the Indian Airlines aircraft to Lahore on 29 September 1981. It also claimed responsibility for the killings of Lala Jagat Narain and Shri Atwal, deputy inspector general of police. The Dal Khalsa regards Pakistan as a strategic ally. It was declared unlawful on 1 May 1982.

The Akhand Kirtani Jatha extends support to other Sikh political and extremist organizations, particularly the Babbar Khalsa. The Babbar Khalsa also looks to Pakistan for support. Its activists have been talking about plans to organize a Khalistan Liberation army.

These organizations, though insignificant in themselves, have obviously been functioning as conduits for assistance from external sources. They have also played an important role in presenting a distorted picture on developments in India to the Sikhs settled abroad.

IV
ARMY ACTION IN PUNJAB AND THE UNION TERRITORY OF CHANDIGARH

On 2 June 1984 the army was called in aid of civil authority in Punjab and was given the task of checking and controlling extremist, terrorist and communal violence.

The army's plan to re-establish law and order envisaged apprehension of terrorist elements, the flushing out of known terrorist hideouts, recovery of illegal arms and ammunition and restoration of public safety and confidence.

To save the situation from irretrievable deterioration, there was utmost necessity for speed in the completion of army operations. Information was available about the accumulation of large quantities of arms of different kinds in different gurdwaras in the state and in the Golden Temple complex where strong fortifications had been built up. Troops were ordered to use the minimum force, to show the utmost reverence to all holy places and to ensure that no desecration or damage was done to the Harmandir Sahib and the Darbar Sahibs of other gurdwaras. Commanders were instructed to use the public address systems to advise terrorists to give themselves up in order to prevent bloodshed and damage to holy places.

The dispositions of the terrorists in the Golden Temple area were organized on military lines. The Akal Takht had been chosen as a building of prime importance since it housed Shri Bhindranwale and his headquarters and was tactically significant to their operations. The approaches to the Akal Takht were heavily defended. The open space to its east had been developed as a 'killing ground' with effective fire being brought down on it from all sides.

The Akal Takht had been fortified as well as any dugout position of any modern army. Starting from the basement upwards, gun placements had been planned out and sited at every level including the floor level, the window level, the roof ventilators, on to the first floor and the upper storeys. The terrorists had cut holes in the walls and the marble facade like a pillbox for the positioning of weapons.

The terrorists had received extensive training in military operations and use of explosives and sophisticated weapons, installed their own communication systems and stored adequate quantities of foodgrains to last several months. They were as well trained and equipped as any regular force could be.

During the afternoon and evening of 5 June 1984 repeated appeals were made to the terrorists to lay down their arms; 129 persons surrendered. At 1900 hours on 5 June, the army commenced preliminary operations to move towards the Golden Temple precincts. The terrorists unleashed deadly and concentrated volume of machine-gun fire from the Akal Takht and from Harmandir Sahib. The troops suffered heavy casualties but showed great restraint and refrained from directing any firing at Harmandir Sahib.

At 0100 hrs. on 6 June, Sant Harchand Singh Longowal and Shri G.S. Tohra surrendered near Guru Nanak Niwas with about 350 people. The terrorists opened fire at them, killing 70 people including 30 women and 5 children.

At about 0410 hrs. on 6 June, anti-tank rockets were fired from the Akal Takht, immobilizing an armoured personnel carrier (APC). Thereafter one tank with its searchlights was taken into the area to blind the terrorist positions in the Akal Takht and to engage these with fire. After the machine-gun positions of the Akal Takht had been silenced, room-to-room engagement commenced. The terrorists ran down towards the first and ground floors where shortly thereafter an explosion took place and a fire started. The Akal Takht was cleared by 1230 hrs. on 6 June, except for resistance from the ground floor and basements.

On the afternoon of 6 June, 200 terrorists surrendered including 22 from Harmandir Sahib. The ground floor and the basement of the Akal Takht was tackled during the night of 6/7 June. A thorough search of the ground floor and of the basement revealed the bodies of Shri Bhindranwale and Shri Amrik Singh among 34 other bodies on the ground floor.

The army took heavy casualties in order to ensure that the Harmandir Sahib and Akal Takht were not damaged. Fire on the Akal Takht had to be opened only when very high casualties began to accrue and when the terrorists started using anti-tank weapons from this building.

A large quantity of weapons, ammunition and explosives was recovered, including automatic and anti-tank weapons. A small factory for the manufacture of hand grenades and Sten guns was also found within the precincts of the Golden Temple.

A total number of 42 religious places were identified where terrorists were based. The army moved into those premises in stages to flush them out. It encountered a fair amount of resistance in the gurdwaras at Moga and Muktsar. The terrorists also fired in Faridkot, Patiala, Ropar and Chowk Mehta. Major recovery of arms and ammunition was made from religious places at Chowk Mehta, Patiala and Ropar. The last of these operations was completed by 1700 hours on 6 June.

The army is still engaged in the process of recovery of arms and of apprehending terrorists who have spread out all over the state.

Details of civilian and army casualties and of arms and ammunition recovered up to June 30 1984 are given in Annexure XI of the White Paper.

V
SOME ISSUES

By about the middle of 1983, antinational and terrorist groups had established complete control over the Golden Temple and converted it as the main base for their operations. The large quantities of weapons of offensive character and communication equipment and the arms factory discovered from the temple fully bear out their ultimate objective, namely, full-scale insurgency. Any delay on the part of the government in breaking these well-entrenched bastions of terrorists and secessionists would have been disastrous for the whole country. The events in Punjab have raised some vital issues:

Is it right for places of worship which are revered by millions to be used as arsenals?

Is it right to transform such places into sanctuaries for criminals and subversive elements?

How do we prevent the secular foundations of our republic from being eroded?

It is inconceivable that the Akali Dal and the SGPC were not aware of the open desecration and misuse of the holy precints of the Golden Temple, but no voice was raised against this by them. Can the SGPC which has the legal responsibility for the management of these religious shrines plead ignorance and absolve itself of the responsibility for their misuse? The Golden Temple and other gurdwaras were used to provide total immunity to criminals and to those who worked to disrupt the unity of the country.

The recent occurrences in Punjab cannot be divorced from the wider international context. Powerful forces are at work to undermine India's political and economic strength. A sensitive border state with a dynamic record of agricultural and industrial development would be an obvious target for subversion. Repeated external aggression and other pressures having failed to break the unity of India, attempts are now being made to cause internal disruption, pressing religion into service.

Other questions are being posed:

(i) How is it that sophisticated weapons in such large quantities managed to get inside the Golden Temple and other gurdwaras?

(ii) Was not the government aware that such arsenals were being built up inside the Golden Temple and other gurdwaras? Was there not a failure of intelligence?

(iii) Was there any support from foreign countries and sources available to the terrorists?

Intelligence on the quantity and type of arms acquired by the terrorists as well as their intentions and strategy of action was broadly correct. The arms and ammunition were smuggled into the Golden Temple and other gurdwaras in '*kar seva*' and other vehicles which used to carry foodstuffs and other materials. They were also smuggled in by terrorists, mixing with pilgrim crowds in the temple. However, the ground information was weak. For instance, while the government knew about the plans of terrorists to sabotage railway tracks and to stage dramatic action against railway stations, exact locations and the particular gangs to be deployed for attacks were not known. While serious acts of sabotage were detected, actual attacks on small and isolated flag stations could not be prevented.

As for the supply of arms, initially the terrorists got them through surprise raids on armouries and through occasional snatching from the police personnel. More sophisticated arms were obtained through sources outside the country. More facts will be available when investigations are completed. There is, however, no doubt that the main distribution centre of arms to the terrorist gangs was based in the Golden Temple.

The government have reason to believe that the terrorists were receiving different types of active support from certain foreign sources. However, it would not be in the public interest to divulge such information.

The action which the government has had to take in Punjab was neither against the Sikhs nor the Sikh religion; it was against terrorism and insurgency. The Sikh community stands firm, along with the rest of the nation, in its resolve to preserve and strengthen the unity and integrity of the country.

Even after the tragic events outlined in the foregoing pages, the government remains committed to its stand that a lasting solution should be found through the democratic process of discussion. For this an atmosphere of peace, mutual trust and accommodation is necessary. In any settlement there has to be give and take, and above all, a commitment to the basic concept that the country's interests always come above the interests of a state or group.

It is government's sincere hope that all sections of the people will contribute to the creation of an atmosphere of trust and amity.

About the Contributors

Amarjit Kaur was a Member of Parliament and was closely associated with the Government of India's efforts in bringing about an understanding between the two communities in Punjab.

Lt Gen Jagjit Singh Aurora, PVSM, who successfully led the Bangladesh operations in 1971, was one of the most capable ex-Army officers to analyze the planning and execution of Operation Bluestar.

Khushwant Singh, veteran journalist, prolific writer and former Member of Parliament, is the author of a definitive two-volume history of the Sikhs, and one of the best-remembered novels on the partition of India, *Train to Pakistan.*

M.V. Kamath, also a veteran journalist and Khushwant Singh's successor as the editor of the erstwhile *Illustrated Weekly of India,* is one of the few writers who has been able to take an objective stand on the army action in Punjab during Operation Bluestar.

Shekhar Gupta, currently Editor-in-Chief of *The Indian Express,* was one of the few journalists to have witnessed Operation Bluestar in action. Here he provides a firsthand account of the army action.

Subhash Kirpekar remained in Amritsar during Operation Bluestar. He interviewed Giani Kirpal Singh and Baba Santa Singh of the Buddha Dal who performed *kar seva* in the Golden Temple complex.

Sunil Sethi hails from the city of Amritsar in Punjab, a state which he covered extensively in his years as a journalist. As a Punjabi himself, he has felt and described best the great divide between the communities. He is now a leading TV anchor with New Delhi Television (NDTV).

Tavleen Singh, leading columnist and political commentator, was the only journalist at the time to have interviewed each extremist leader of Punjab.